MW00582989

Enjoy: Luxury of Life

Your Secret Keys to
Global Giving & World Wealth

Thank You Harry, Enjoy Luxury of Life

[signature]

All Rights Reserved
© 2009 by Joy Macci PhD & Alexandria Hilton MA

This book may not be reproduced in whole or in part, by any means, without written consent of the publisher.

LIFESUCCESS PUBLISHING, LLC
8900 E Pinnacle Peak Road, Suite D240
Scottsdale, AZ 85255

Telephone: 800.473.7134
Fax: 480.661.1014
E-mail: admin@lifesuccesspublishing.com

ISBN (hardcover):   978-1-59930-249-2
ISBN (ebook):   978-1-59930-250-8

Cover :   Daniela A. Savone, LifeSuccess Publishing, LLC
Text: Daniela A. Savone, LifeSuccess Publishing, LLC
Edited by: Publications Services, Inc.

COMPANIES, ORGANIZATIONS, INSTITUTIONS, AND INDUSTRY PUBLICATIONS: Quantity discounts are available on bulk purchases of this book for reselling, educational purposes, subscription incentives, gifts, sponsorship, or fundraising. Special books or book excerpts can also be created to fit specific needs such as private labeling with your logo on the cover and a message from a VIP printed inside. For more information, please contact our Special Sales Department at LifeSuccess Publishing, LLC.

Printed in Canada.

Enjoy: Luxury of Life

Your Secret Keys to
Global Giving & World Wealth

JOY MACCI PhD &
ALEXANDRIA HILTON MA

Dedication

May you discover and Enjoy the true Luxury of Life
with Global Giving … and pass it on!

Contents

Your Invitation

Each and every one of us comes to a point in our life where we stop and think, "What am I doing with my life? Am I living my divine purpose? What's important now and where do I go from here? Have I fully developed my God-given talents and reached my highest levels of love, success, health, and wealth?" And, most importantly, "How can I fully enjoy the emotional benefits of knowing I touched the lives of others and leave a lasting legacy for my family, friends and loved ones to emulate?"

The natural tendency is to look around one's own backyard for opportunities to help improve the lives of others. This is a noble and valid desire, but often we have more to offer or give. As our world continuously shrinks and the vast chasms between cultures and turbulent areas of the world are laid bare, so to are the needs of individuals. The current crisis within our global economy underscores the fragility of those that live at the very door of poverty and despair. Though our languages, cultures, and perspectives may be different, we are all living together on this planet and feel a strong kinship to our fellow human beings no matter their religious leanings or political systems.

Many people throughout the world today have time, talent, and resources on a scale that will enable them to not only share with others around them, but to literally change the world. The lasting legacy of any person of wealth is to leave the world a better place for their having lived. This is possible by generously giving time and resources to effect change and improvement in the lives of individuals and communities around the globe.

With this idea in mind, we chose to profile some of the best-known philanthropists of the past in our Global Giving Hall of Fame. This elite group includes such humanitarian leaders as Andrew Carnegie, Mahatma Gandhi, Princess Diana, and our 2008 Global Giving Award Winner, Paul Newman. We also want to honor those who are carrying on this great mission today. The Ambassadors of Global Giving showcases current leaders for whom philanthropy is a way of life. Their extraordinary efforts are changing the world we know and offering hope for a better tomorrow.

We also realize the importance of teaching the next generation the principles of giving through wealth and improving their world. To this end, we created "Alexander's Royal Journey"—a fantasy of discovery for one young man that teaches the most important aspects of philanthropy. This is a story for all ages and generations to share and pass on to others.

Enjoy: Luxury of Life unveils the secret keys to unlock and expand your life, heart, and soul to an exciting Life of Luxury, World Wealth, and Global Giving. Enjoyment (Inner Joy) leads to giving, giving leads to greatness, greatness leads to World Wealth, and World Wealth leads to Legacy Leaders!

When we learn to give, we start to live;
Everything we give away enriches lives day by day.

The ability to embrace our world and foster change on a global scale is unique, requiring passion and a mind-set of personal responsibility. Those individuals are rare and gifted in their understanding of the human condition and their ability to effectively use their wealth for the greatest good. We invite you to join us. Begin your own journey of fulfillment and true happiness through the world of Global Giving.

We are passing the secret keys to
World Wealth and Global Giving to you.
Your mission is to pass it on.

Thank you for joining us on this noble life journey,

Joy Macci PhD & Alexandria Hilton MA

Introduction to the World & the Secret Keys

Welcome to the World of Global Giving as we unveil the Secret Keys of Life, Luxury and Legacy! The greatest philanthropists of our time knew that we are not measured by what we accumulate in this life, but by what we give and the legacy we leave behind.

These philanthropists include the likes of Andrew Carnegie, Princess Diana, and Paul Newman. They knew the secret keys to creating a long-lasting legacy that has and will impact generations of people. They, and many others, embody the spirit of Global Giving and the ability to encourage others to follow their lead in creating a better existence for others.

Today, all over the world, wonderful philanthropic endeavors are underway to improve the lives of people in various and distinct ways. Join us now as we journey through countries and continents and learn of some of the wonderful and fascinating endeavors you can take part in on your own quest to becoming a Global Giver.

I think the great livers, the people who are fully self-actualizing and alive, are the great givers.

—**Mark Victor Hansen**

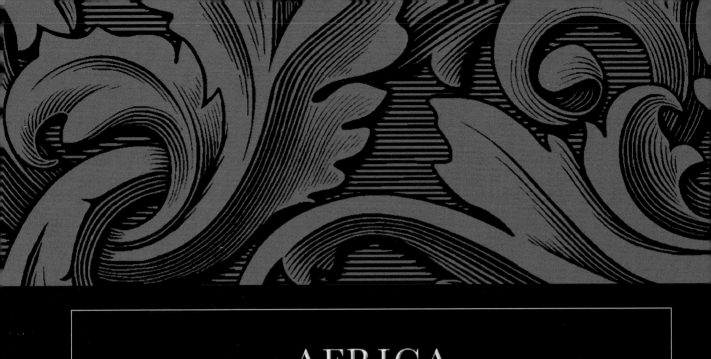

AFRICA

*Wealth is not to feed our egos, but
to feed the hungry and to help
people help themselves.*

—Andrew Carnegie

AFRICA HUMANITARIAN ACTION (ETHIOPIA)

Africa Humanitarian Action (AHA) was founded in 1994 as a nongovernmental organization that provides humanitarian assistance by "building on the strength of African people to solve African problems." Originally created in response to the Rwandan genocide, AHA has since supported more than nine million people in sixteen African countries. AHA employs more than 1,400 staff members, 85 percent of whom are recruited from local communities, bringing not only the knowledge and experience needed for success, but also important community ties. By recruiting from within the community, AHA is better able to address the problems facing the continent.

AHA addresses a variety of needs, and by working in partnership with the local populations, also empowers people to make a long-term difference in their own lives. The organization believes that a participatory approach is the only way that real change can be achieved.

www.africahumanitarianaction.org

Life begets life. Energy becomes energy. It is by spending oneself that one becomes rich.

—Sarah Bernhardt

GROOTBOS PRIVATE GAME RESERVE (SOUTH AFRICA)

The Grootbos Private Game Reserve looks to blend environmental and social activism. The foundation is dedicated to the preservation of native landscapes, as well as to the training local people to make a living in the same manner. One example of this blend in action is the Green Futures College, originally funded by both the Grootbos Foundation and a grant from the German government. The Green Futures College trains locals in natural and sustainable livelihoods such as horticulture, ecotourism, and landscaping. The college is now self-supporting with a landscaping and nursery business that also employs many of its graduates. The students learn a livelihood and life skills, such as using a bank account, using the Internet, and getting a driver's license.

Grootbos has a five-star rating and private luxury suites. There are two lodges for guests, each with very different experiences. The Garden Lodge is billed as an ideal family getaway, set in a lush and indigenous surrounding. The Forest Lodge, on the other hand, is more contemporary and modern. The De Kelders cliffs, practically at the Lodge's doorstep, offer unparalleled land-based whale viewing within thirty meters of the shoreline.

www.grootbos.com

Charity sees the need,

not the cause.

—**Proverb**

HEIFER INTERNATIONAL (EAST AFRICA)

Heifer International believes that the root of many environmental problems is poverty, a claim that necessitates a holistic approach in building sustainable communities. In times of need, people often make decisions based on a lack of alternatives. This organization is working on a system of practices that will provide what people need, while also enhancing environmental quality and the use of natural resources.

Communities need to learn how to protect their resources and how to rejuvenate their land, water, and other natural resources. Heifer helps teach environmentally sound techniques that address this need. Every project through Heifer contains an environmental aspect to help families work toward restoring a balanced ecology. Heifer teaches families how to keep their land healthy, not only for their own use but for future generations, such as planting techniques that better resist erosion.

Heifer International claims that, from their experience, 70 percent of the world's poor and two-thirds of the world's illiterate are women. Women own only 1 percent of the world's property. Meanwhile, women produce from 55 percent of the world's food up to 80 percent in some areas of the world. One of Heifer's goals is to bring more visibility to women and their role in the fight against poverty. The organization offers microenterprise loans and no-interest living loans in the form of livestock to help families start and expand businesses. Heifer International also works with HIV/AIDS education organizations and the Young People's Initiative to empower youth with the skills and opportunities necessary to create positive life changes.

www.heifer.org

I've always said that the better off you are, the more responsibility you have for helping others.

—Carlos Slim Helu

THE AMERICAS

*I have found that among its
other benefits, giving liberates
the soul of the giver.*

—Maya Angelou

COOPA-ROCA (BRAZIL)

Rocinha's Craftwork and Sewing Cooperative, or COOPA-ROCA, was created in the 1980s by Maria Teresa Leal. The co-op members are women ranging in age from eighteen to sixty-five, most of whom are homemakers with no income previous to their involvement in COOPA-ROCA. Leal's goal was to allow women, many single mothers, from the poorest Rio de Janeiro neighborhood to obtain flexible employment that would allow them to improve their income without having to leave home. Many of the women are skilled seamstresses, but they had no way to use their skills for income. Leal founded a sewing cooperative in Rocinha, the largest *favela* (slum) in Rio de Janeiro, in 1981.

The women used fabric remnants and traditional Brazilian techniques (*fuxico*, or embroidering with pieces of fabric, crochet, patchwork, drawstring appliqué, and knot work) to create decorative crafts, quilts, and pillows. Leal arranged for donations of luxury fabrics from factories, and the pieces created by the co-op gained notoriety as traditional craftsmanship combined with couture fashion. She also arranged for the group to meet with designers to learn developing fashion trends. Now the group is partnered with Brazilian designers Carlos Miele, Osklen, M.Officer, Eliza Conde, Amazonlife, Dautore, and the department store C&A, as well as British designer Paul Smith and French designers Ann Taylor and Le Bon Marche. COOPA-ROCA members attend a wide variety of shows to see their own creations on models in Rio de Janeiro, São Paulo, London, Milan, and Berlin.

www.coopa-roca.org.br

How wonderful it is that nobody

needs to wait a single moment before

starting to improve the world.

—Anne Frank

PLAYA VIVA RESORT (MEXICO)

Playa Viva is moving beyond the word sustainability, past the ordinary ideas of eco-friendly materials and conservation, and into the new concept of regeneration. The idea is not just conservation, but to genuinely improve everything you use, to consistently strengthen the entire ecosystem. The resort contributes to healthier water, soil, and air, and extends those benefits not only to guests, but also to the surrounding environment and communities. It is described as eco-fantasy or natural luxury.

Located on the west coast of Mexico in the town of Juluchuca, Playa Viva, a forty-room beach hotel and spa, boasts such innovations as an on-site turtle sanctuary, one of the largest in Mexico, where remnant turtle eggs are crushed and mixed with local materials for wall plaster; tree house casitas that are suspended between living palm trees to protect against beach erosion; and biodiesel-converted coconut oil that is used to power on-site vehicles. A large portion of the resort, 160 acres, has been designated a nature preserve; additionally, there is a large amount of surrounding organic farmland. Through their focus on the community, Playa Viva has gone beyond being merely environmentally friendly by genuinely investing in the well-being of the local community, improving and strengthening the area in many ways.

Founders David Levanthal and Sandra Kahn, as well as an entire team of designers and developers, are not only concerned with the environment, but also the local communities. When they have offered training to the residents on organic practices to move away from pesticides, improve water quality, and recycle trash and plastics, they haven't just dumped the information and walked away. The Playa Viva team established a Community Supported Agriculture program to help farmers find and create markets for organically grown produce. Playa Viva also helped to create local recycling centers and is currently helping the local salt co-op reimagine its product, much as they did for the candy factories in Juluchuca, redesigning the product and packaging, reducing costs, and searching for healthier alternatives to corn syrup.

www.playaviva.com

*We make a living by
what we get, we make a life
by what we give.*

—Winston Churchill

Happiest are the people who give
most happiness to others.

—Dennis Diderot

Toskan Casale Foundation (Canada)

The Toskan Casale Foundation was formed in 2001 by the joint founders of M·A·C Cosmetics: Julie Toskan-Casale, Victor Casale, and Frank Toskan. The foundation supports community-based organizations that offer not only short-term assistance, but also long-term solutions and stability.

Julie managed the M·A·C AIDS Fund while employed with M·A·C Cosmetics. She became the first Canadian graduate from the Rockefeller Foundation's Philanthropy Workshop in 1999. Then, in 2001, she created the Toskan Casale Foundation and followed that by developing the Youth and Philanthropy Initiative in 2002. The Youth and Philanthropy Initiative provides high school students the chance to participate in a philanthropy program to actively change their communities for the better and to practice a leadership position. It has donated over $2,500,000 through its students since its inception, proving that today's youth, typically dismissed and untapped, can perform beyond expectations. The objective of the program is to prepare youth to effectively change their world.

The Youth and Philanthropy Initiative is presented to students in the ninth and tenth grades, free of charge. The students learn about philanthropy and research local issues, each class choosing one charity from many candidates. The students then present proposals for funding their charities to a panel, and one finalist is chosen to receive $5,000 from the Toskan Casale Foundation. These students have proven that youth can bring a new sense of inspiration and drive to affect the problems they see in their own communities. As the foundation states, "Combining classroom learning with practical community experience, the students will gain skills in the art of researching grassroots organizations, proposal writing, public speaking, evaluation, analysis and logical decision-making."

www.toskanfoundation.org

Education is the most powerful weapon which you can use to change the world.

—Nelson Mandela

YACHANA LODGE (ECUADOR)

Yachana Lodge was built in Ecuador in 1995. Thirteen years later, the lodge is an award-winning tourism destination. Yachana Lodge is the Condé Nast Best Ecotourism Lodge in the World (2004), World Travel and Tourism Council Investor in People Award finalist (2006), and the Ashoka and National Geographic Geotourism Challenge winner (2008).

In the indigenous Kichua, *yachana* means "a place for learning." The Yachana Lodge has founded a technical high school; Yachana Gourmet, the producer of Yachana Jungle Chocolate; a clinic; and a nature preserve to better the local community. The high school offers classes in agriculture, animal husbandry, culinary arts, conservation, microenterprise, and ecotourism, to provide a practical education for the youth in the community. The school's students are primarily indigenous and come from families who earn an average of $300 per year. The school also offers internships at the hotel in a variety of areas related to the school's studies.

The nature preserve is over 4,300 acres of rainforest, a number that continues to grow as the Yachana Lodge purchases land. All of Yachana Lodge's land was officially declared a protected forest in 2002 by the Ecuadorian Ministry of Environment. Guests are welcome to visit the protected rainforest, which also serves as a living classroom for the high school.

The lodge offers travelers a chance to not only experience, but to contribute to the area's continued success and enrichment. Yachana Lodge believes "the future of the rainforest is inextricably linked to the well-being of its inhabitants; only those who call the rainforest their home can ensure its survival."

www.yachana.com

The great use of life is to spend it for something that will outlast it.

—William James

ASIA

*If you want to change the
world, be that change.*

—Mahatma Gandhi

AASARA (INDIA)

Aasara is an organization that works for the street children in India. This agency offers a wide array of services: formal and nonformal education, vocational training (computers, carpentry, tailoring, embroidery, housekeeping, and gardening are among the trades offered), health care and medical aid, nutritional care, personal and group counseling, recreation opportunities, job placement, social rehabilitation, and reunification with family. Aasara rehabilitates some fifty children per year, and reunites perhaps twenty-five with their families. Aasara achieves all this through day-care centers, with more complete care at residential shelters. There are shelters specific to boys, such as the Digha boy's shelter, and girls, the Suraksha Crisis Shelter.

Aasara's goal is to advocate for street children and to address the social, physical, and emotional needs that will allow them to become productive and well-adjusted members of society who can educate the public about their issues. They have gone beyond simply sustaining the children by making them self-reliant. Aasara specializes in catering to the individual, nurturing talents, and giving meaning to lives.

www.aasara.com

'Tis not enough to help the feeble
up but to support him after.

—William Shakespeare

Aavishkaar (India)

Aavishkaar is a micro-venture capital fund that promotes start-ups that will impact rural and semi-urban development in India. Micro-venture capital invests in small projects that generally elude the investment of venture capitalists, but carry too much risk to attain traditional lending support. Aavishkaar provides anywhere from $20,000 to $500,000 to these groups, but, beyond financial support, they also provide management support and professional expertise necessary to take a company from grassroots to thriving enterprise.

Aavishkaar is looking for leaders to help create the environment of success for these innovative businesses. Success from these businesses can help change the financial landscape for India's rural and semi-urban areas. A successful society depends on its ability to change and innovate and, more importantly, on its ability to sustain that innovation.

www.aavishkaar.org

That best portion of a good man's life:

His little, nameless, unremembered acts

of kindness and of love.

—**William Wordsworth**

ACTIONAID (CHINA)

ActionAid China works in poverty-stricken communities with such services as the construction of water wells, irrigation canals, hydropowered rice mills, and road paving. They also focus on gender equality and train women in reproductive health. Poor and marginalized groups are trained and encouraged to improve their own daily living conditions, improve self-management, and articulate their concerns. The agency began in 1998, when ActionAid signed a ten-year Memorandum of Understanding with China's Ministry of Science and Technology to work together in China for poverty reduction. As of 2007, ActionAid China operates in 186 villages in five provinces.

ActionAid China's vision is "a harmonious society without poverty, inequality, and injustice in which every person can exercise his or her rights with dignity." ActionAid's five intervention areas are the rights to food and livelihood for farmers and migrant workers, education for rural children, HIV/AIDS prevention and support, disaster preparedness, and women's rights. The agency is working toward an environmentally sensitive, sustainable economy for the poor and women's equal opportunity in education, employment, and political participation.

The major groups that ActionAid China has identified and is working with are women, rural farmers, migrants, and ethnic groups. Among the poor, women are the marginalized group, far more vulnerable to poverty than men. The farmers fall into several groups, each with their own rights issues: subsistence farmers, cash-crop farmers, livestock raisers, and landless farmers. The number of migrant workers has been increasing in the cities. These workers often take low-paying work in insecure work environments and are unable to share the same privileges as the urban residents in terms of employment, education, job security, and timely pay. In ethnic populations, fifty-five minority groups account for 7 percent of China's population, generally located in rural areas, and those families are marginalized in educational, cultural, and economic issues.

LITTLE SUNSHINE TEACHERS

One program started by ActionAid China began when the women's activity centers were established in two villages in Zhangjiachuan. Ten local children were given the position of Little Sunshine Teachers. These children were to take what they learned in school home to teach their mothers. In Zhangjiachuan, 70 percent of the population is Hui Muslim and the women's illiteracy rate is over 90 percent, as local customs limit women's opportunities in education. The Little Sunshine program complements the services of the women's center, which teaches women to write, offers training, and gives women a place to gather to discuss women's issues in the community.

www.actionaid.org/china

*It is a kingly act to
assist the fallen.*

—Mother Teresa

*Life's persistent and most
urgent question is "What are
you doing for others?"*

—Martin Luther King, Jr.

GOLDEN TRIANGLE RESORT (THAILAND)

This resort offers the natural beauty, charms, and enchantment of Thailand in fifty-eight guest rooms and an additional nineteen suites. Truly a luxury, the resort is nestled in 160 acres of Thai jungle. There is an elephant camp on-site, and opportunities to experience the local culture with a cooking school, visits to local villages, border markets, and boat rides. The entire experience immerses the guest in nature, local culture and heritage, and adventure.

The Anantara Golden Triangle Resort is also known as one of the most socially responsible hotels in the world, one of only ten chosen by *Forbes Traveler*. The elephant sanctuary houses almost thirty elephants, giving each a respite from the out-of-work conditions that other elephants in the region suffer. Because many elephants were trained to work in the logging industry, which was banned in the '80s, and in the cities, elephants banned from working are often used by people to beg for money and frequently live in poor conditions. Because the elephant population in Thailand is dwindling, 1,500 wild and 2,500 domesticated, the elephant camp at the resort is not simply entertainment: it is conservation at work. Of course, bringing in the elephants means bringing in their trainers, or *mahouts*, who also have families. The resort houses them all and provides housing, school, and medical treatment. The resort also gives the *mahout* wives an opportunity to sell their crafts for extra income at the hotel gift shop, where the women keep 100 percent of the profit from the sales.

http://goldentriangle.anantara.com

Words mean nothing.
Action is the only thing. Doing.
That's the only thing.

—Ernest Gaines

HÔTEL DE LA PAIX (CAMBODIA)

Hôtel de la Paix offers visitors the chance not only to experience Cambodia's natural beauty and local culture, but also to directly affect the lives of Cambodian people for the better. Those who are fortunate enough are given the opportunity to help those who are not, while both benefit from the exchange of culture and respect. The hotel's team cultivates local connections and keeps tabs on the needs of the surrounding communities.

Hôtel de la Paix also works with several orphanages in the area: the Sangkeum Centre for Children, the Sunrise Angkor Children's Village, Missionaries of Charity, and the Children's Development Village.

Guests are offered a variety of ways to contribute. One option is to purchase a six-month training course for a student through the Hôtel de la Paix Sewing Training Centre. Another option is to sponsor a child through the Life and Hope Association; when guests sponsor children, they help to provide school uniforms and school supply kits. There is a rice sponsorship, in which a guest can purchase a ton of rice to donate to local orphanages.

Rice sponsorships are also arranged for individual families in outlying villages. The Shinta Mani Institute offers training and community assistance programs. The Green Gecko Project offers hotel patrons an opportunity to provide local children with personal hygiene kits containing a toothbrush, toothpaste, soap, soap container, hairbrush, facecloth, and towel. Other hotel-supported community projects include: the Sihanouk Hospital Center of Hope, which provides education and training in the medical field, as well as free quality medical care for the needy, and the Sangkheum Centre for Children, which provides education and training in agriculture, traditional dance, cuisine, and sports. Guests can contribute the money to build a home for a local family and even arrange to be there at completion. In addition, purchases of water wells, vegetable seeds, and agricultural training, as well as a pair of piglets to raise and breed, can also be arranged.

www.hoteldelapaixangkor.com

Many persons have a wrong idea of what constitutes true happiness. It is not attained through self-gratification but through fidelity to a worthy purpose.

—Helen Keller

If you want to lift yourself up,

lift up someone else.

—Booker T. Washington

NIHIWATU (INDONESIA)

Nihiwatu is a small and very exclusive island resort on the secluded Sumba Island in eastern Indonesia. Claude Graves and his wife, Petra, built the resort with an eye toward responsible tourism, creating a resort that gives more than it takes. Nihiwatu offers a great deal to its guests, but offers even more to the local community.

Nihiwatu is two-and-a-half kilometers of absolutely private and protected beachfront, as well as 175 hectares of idyllic and peaceful tropical retreat varied between forest, grasslands, and rice terraces. Since 1989, the resort has helped build six area schools and seven medical clinics. Two hundred villages now have clean water, and the local economy has been stimulated. Nihiwatu sources much of its building materials and food locally, and 95 percent of the staff is local as well.

The resort takes great care to minimize its environmental impact as well. Its carbon footprint is offset by a plan to plant over 160,000 trees over seven years; all waste is composted, recycled, and sold; and the generators are powered with coconut oil bio-diesel, which cuts resort emissions by 75 percent.

www.nihiwatu.com

No piled-up wealth, no social station, no throne, reaches as high as that spiritual plane upon which every human being stands by virtue of his humanity.

—Edwin Hubbell Chapin

SECOND HARVEST JAPAN (JAPAN)

Second Harvest Japan is the first food bank in Japan, where more then 650,000 people lack access to safe and nutritious food through "socially acceptable channels." Often food with damaged labels or packaging is thrown away. This food can instead be given to a food bank, saving disposal costs for the company who cannot sell the food that is otherwise fine, and offering a social service at the same time. In Japan, the cost associated with disposing food is 100 yen per kilogram, but now Second Harvest helps companies save time, money, and labor by picking it up for free. The food bank ensures that the food will not end up in the market again, delivers the food to the homeless in Tokyo every week, and works with various sources for distribution.

Hiroshi Fujita started the process in January 2000 after seeing the success and effectiveness of a recent rice drive. July 24, 2002, the Tokyo Metropolitan Government officially approved the food bank, then called Food Bank Japan, as Japan's first legally incorporated nonprofit food bank. Second Harvest Japan distributes its food to soup kitchens, orphanages, and emergency shelters, as well as to the homeless, single mothers, migrant workers, and many others.

www.secondharvestjapan.org

I shall pass through this world but once.
Any good therefore that I can do or any
kindness that I can show to any human being,
let me do it now. Let me not defer or neglect it,
for I shall not pass this way again.

—**Mahatma Gandhi**

VIL UYANA (SRI LANKA)

Built on a man-made wetland habitat, this Sri Lankan resort is the first with dwellings built over water and rice paddy fields, the first man-made lakes created in centuries. Vil Uyana also plans to build forested areas over reclaimed agricultural land. Additional social responsibility comes in the form of job training. In 2006, Vil Uyana started a youth development program that prepares young people for employment in hospitality and related fields. They provide classes in both the English and Japanese languages, office skills, culinary training, and wildlife guiding. The youth development project won the Pacific Asia Travel Association (PATA) Grand Award in 2007 for education and training.

www.jetwing.com

There is a natural law, a divine law that obliges you and me to relieve the suffering, the distressed and the destitute.

—Conrad Hilton

EUROPE

The future belongs to
those who believe in the beauty
of their dreams.

—Eleanor Roosevelt

Caja Navarra (Spain)

Caja Navarra is a bank that operates on an idea called *civic banking*. The bank is organized as a foundation and donates 30 percent of its profits to charities and social projects. Caja Navarra's civic-banking program is called "You Choose: You Decide." Caja Navarra also encourages its customers to volunteer for the projects of their choice. The customer can actually choose the area that will receive the 30 percent donation. The program began officially in 2004 with eight areas of social improvement: disability and welfare, research, cooperation, environment, employment and entrepreneurs, culture, preservation of heritage, and sports and leisure. In 2005, the system was changed so the entire social budget was decided by the bank's customers, and customers receive an individualized report on how much money the bank has donated from their account. The original eight categories have been expanded to include specific projects for customers to choose from, or customers can propose their own projects to be added to the list of over 2,500.

In addition, the bank's branches are not simply a place to conduct business. Caja Navarra calls them *canchas*, and this space allows not only business, but also children's play areas, free public Internet access, free coffee, community meeting rooms, and even live entertainment once a week.

www.cajanavarra.es

*Do your duty and a little more and
the future will take care of itself.*

—Andrew Carnegie

Edun (Ireland)

Edun is an Irish-based fashion label founded by Ali Hewson; her husband, Bono; and Rogan Gregory in 2005. The company is socially conscious, offering employment in developing countries through a micro approach to manufacturing. Offering employment and trade and bringing business and income to the areas that need it most is seen as far more effective support for communities, rather than simply offering money or goods for nothing.

Edun also works toward the use of more organic materials. All their T-shirts are made from 100 percent organic cotton, which provides a healthier condition for workers and a socially and environmentally responsible choice for the buyer. Edun is a complete collection, not just popular T-shirts. The collection is created in various developing countries (India, Peru, Tunisia, Kenya, Uganda, Lesotho, Mauritius, and Madagascar) and sold around the globe.

www.edunonline.com

No individual has any right to come into the world and go out of it without leaving behind him distinct and legitimate reasons for having passed through it.

—George Washington Carver

MONACO YACHT SHOW (MONACO)

Since 2005, the Monaco Yacht Show (MYS) has been carbon neutral. Each of the last three years has successfully negated the carbon footprint that the show itself creates. After evaluating the emissions used by exhibitors and visitors, transportation, hotel stays, electricity, and the yachts (including yacht transportation and related waste), the MYS contributed an ecology tax over those three years to help fund other international environmental projects.

The MYS has invested nearly 150,000 euros in sustainable development. The show bought carbon offsets to purchase wind turbines in 2007 and also contributed to other ecologically sound projects. The MYS has been associated with creating wind-turbine sites in Northern China, New Zealand, and India. The show also had a presence in Scotland and France with reforestation projects and in Pennsylvania with a coal mining methane-capture system.

These efforts have shown that luxury and eco-friendly lifestyles can exist together, and there are current plans to build a new island near the Fontvielle harbor. The project must be environmentally friendly, a floating island that will prevent any damage to the local marine ecology, and provide additional housing property for residents. The new island will house hotels, apartments, a university, and a museum.

www.monacoyachtshow.com

We are here to add what we can to life,

not to get what we can from it.

—William Osler

MIDDLE EAST

Woman, above all other educators,

educated humanity ... woman is the

heart of humanity.

—Samuel Smiles

COMMITTEE TO DEFEND WOMEN'S RIGHTS IN THE MIDDLE EAST (IRAN)

The CDWRME's stance is that the first step toward women's liberation is the separation of religion from state. The committee works for equal gender rights and obligations in such areas as the care of children, family finance, inheritance laws, and divorce and custody issues. CDWRME wants the abolition of honor-killing laws; an end to forced marriage; freedom of clothing for each gender; equal political rights; and the release of restrictions on work, travel, and education for women. The committee fights for severe penalties on family abuse and violence and the prohibition of polygamy.

The committee was founded in 2001 by women's rights activists from Iran, Jordan, and Lebanon. They encourage their supporters to see the difference that one person can make to the victims that the committee helps.

www.middleastwomen.org

The practice of charity will bind us ... will bind all men in one great brotherhood.

—Conrad Hilton

KING FAISAL FOUNDATION (SAUDI ARABIA)

After his death in 1976, King Faisail's eight sons established a foundation in his honor to continue the work that he had done in his life. Faisail's belief was that suffering cannot be eliminated, but, "when people become active rather than passive, it can be relieved." King Faisail was distinguished as the first modern Muslim leader who prioritized the philanthropy that has always been important in Arab traditions. He also introduced women's education despite conservative religious protests.

The King Faisail Foundation emphasizes health, education, research, and Islamic culture. It has funded more than 130 projects all over the world in the form of schools, orphanages, mosques, hospitals and clinics, and agricultural development, taking particular interest in projects with long-term benefits for the communities involved and projects that empower people to help themselves. Most of the foundation's grants go to medical and scientific research.

www.kff.com

I'm not doing my philanthropic work out
of any kind of guilt, or any need to create
good public relations. I'm doing it because
I can afford to do it, and I believe in it.

—George Soros

MOHAMMED BIN RASHID AL MAKTOUM FOUNDATION (UNITED ARAB EMIRATES)

The Sheikh Mohammed bin Rashid Al Maktoum's Foundation was started by a personal endowment of $10 billion with the mission of creating sustainable solutions for particular regional problems. Focusing on knowledge and education, the foundation is working to raise research and higher education to the range of international standards, while also promoting cross-cultural dialogue and participation, fostering respect and mutual understanding among regional cultures.

Illiteracy rates in the Arab world, according to the foundation, range from 20 percent to 40 percent, where 18 percent of that figure are under the age of fifteen and 43 percent are women. These figures illustrate an area of critical need in the region. The foundation is committed to supporting talented and highly educated people and building future leaders.

www.mbrfoundation.ae/English

Stronger women build

stronger nations.

—Women for Women

Women for Women International (Iraq)

Women for Women International was cofounded by Zainab Salbi and Amjad Atallad. Salbi was born in Iraq and emigrated to the United States at the age of nineteen. Her experiences in Iraq exposed her to the worldwide plight of women in war zones. In the 1990s, Atallad and Salbi were newlyweds who gave up their honeymoon in favor of creating an organization that would connect U.S. sponsors with female war survivors. In time, this organization turned into Women for Women International.

In that first year, Women for Women distributed around $9,000, working with eight women. The key to change in women's lives, they found out, was not simply financial assistance. The women needed marketable skills and an emotional lifeline, and they needed to understand their rights and their potential in life. In this way, women could begin to build on their strengths and do more than simply survive. The organization now serves women in many countries: Afghanistan, Bosnia, Herzegovina, Colombia, the Democratic Republic of the Congo, Iraq, Kosovo, Nigeria, Rwanda, and the Sudan. They have one-on-one connections in fifty-five other countries.

Since 1993, the organization has supported female survivors of war in over ten countries, assisting more than 150,000 women and distributing better than $42 million in aid. Beyond that, Women for Women trains women in awareness of rights and supports small business start-ups. The one-year program supports immediate and long-term benefits, changing victims into survivors, and survivors into citizens who actively help to rebuild their nation. In 2006, Women for Women International was the first women's organization to be awarded the Conrad Hilton Humanitarian Award.

www.womenforwomen.org

*Our humanity were a poor
thing but for the divinity
that stirs within us.*

—Francis Bacon

OCEANIA

Is the rich world aware of how four billion of the six billion live? If we were aware, we would want to help out; we'd want to get involved.

—Bill Gates

COALITION AGAINST TRAFFICKING IN WOMEN (AUSTRALIA)

CATWA is the Australian branch of the Coalition Against Trafficking in Women International. The coalition is a women's rights movement that works both locally and internationally to end all forms of exploitation of women: sexual violence, violence in prostitution, trafficking, and pornography. The coalition aims to promote the recognition that trafficking and exploitation are a violation of human rights and to call attention to all forms of sexual exploitation, including trafficking, prostitution, pornography, mail-order brides, incest, and rape. This pro-woman organization is developing strategies to support the women who leave prostitution, supporting the female struggle for dignity and survival both in and out of the sex industry.

www.catwinternational.org

True generosity must benefit both parties. No woman can control her destiny if she doesn't give to herself as much as she gives of herself.

—Suze Orman

Maori Women's Welfare League (New Zealand)

The Maori Women's Welfare League was formed in 1951 in order to "promote fellowship and understanding between Maori and European women and to cooperate with other women's organizations, departments of state, and local bodies for the furtherance of those objects." The league also pledged to maintain, preserve, and perpetuate the Maori culture. The social and political reasons behind the league's formation involved the rapid movement of the Maori from rural districts to urban and the influx of associated problems: housing, health, finance, and racism. A senior welfare officer recognized the need to consult with the women instead of solely the men of the Tribal Committees.

The league's work promotes wellness in the community, centering on home and family life, education, health, housing, and employment. Initiatives have included the promotion of immunization, smoke-free healthy lifestyles, vegetable gardens, and profiling Maori women and the difference they make in their communities. The league has taught car-seat safety and nutrition and created mentoring programs for at-risk students.

*I don't think you ever stop giving.
I really don't. I think it's an on-going
process. And it's not just about being able
to write a check. It's being able to
touch somebody's life.*

—**Oprah Winfrey**

Turtle Island (Fiji)

Richard Evanson bought what amounted to an uninhabited island, five hundred acres of barren land overrun by wild goats, and built what is now an exclusive resort. He employed villagers from nearby communities and planted hundreds of thousands of trees to reverse the damage done to the island. He changed the name from Nanuya Levu to Turtle Island. After granting producers the rights to film Blue Lagoon on his island, Evanson decided to open the property for guests in 1980.

A four-acre hydroponic and organic vegetable garden supplies fresh produce year-round for guests and staff. Turtle Island now employs more than 120 Fijians. Freshwater ponds encourage bird life. A turtle release program has been implemented to help save the threatened Green and Hawksbill turtles. The number of visitors is limited in order to respect the delicate integrity of the island. There are regular medical and dental clinics to treat villagers from neighboring islands. An on-site carpentry department is responsible for making all furniture on the island, as well as items for the gift shop. A secondary school is now in operation on the island to educate the children from seven local villages, which Turtle Island pays for and more than fifty students attend. Evanson's Yasawas Community Foundation generates funds for special projects in the Turtle Island area, and the foundation ensures that the funds collected are applied to projects that matter to the communities themselves, rather than something dictated by outsiders.

www.turtlefiji.com

Learning the Secret Keys

The Secret Keys to Global Giving include many qualities shared by our philanthropy leaders of today and yesterday. The importance of passing these qualities and ideas on to future Global Givers is essential, and we have highlighted them in this delightful tale in order for the Secret Keys to be easily understood and shared with children and loved ones of all ages.

ALEXANDER'S
ROYAL
JOURNEY

Doctissimis Ornatissimisq Viris
D.D. Davidi Sanclaro Antonio de
Willon et D. Martinio Maurelicto
in illustrisi Academia Parisiensi
Professoribus eximiis in vere
smi-citus projudituror D.D.
Petr Kerdius Ao 7645

The boy ducked as the Ming vase came flying across the room, a blur of blue and gold as it barely missed his head before shattering against the wall. The vase was irreplaceable, but Alexander only regretted that he had missed the boy. He was having *another* bad morning. It had started with the morning bath. The water had never been the right temperature. First, it was too hot. The servants had rushed to cool it, but the result had been too cool. Then breakfast had been worse. The boy had tilted the tray while trying to pour hot tea, and everything had crashed onto the table. He was relieved that it hadn't spilled on Alexander, but then a few stray drops hit the fine cloth. Alexander was instantly enraged.

Now, they were upstairs again, in Alexander's room, some ten servants scurrying around to keep him happy. He was changing from his breakfast attire to something for the afternoon, a task which sometimes made him late for lunch. The last thing in a line of Alexander's peeves that day was when he couldn't find his shoes. Now there were shoes flying everywhere, and no one was safe. The first one had missed, but the next shoe found its mark and hit the boy across the cheek. He was dazed and tried desperately not to cry, but Alexander didn't even notice as someone appeared to carry the boy from the room.

Alexander knew he was going to be king. This thought had shaped much of his life. He spent his childhood playing with much different toys than other children his age. Where they might have chewed on carved wooden animals as infants, Alexander had chewed on the ears of tame tigers. Where other children had learned to walk on packed dirt floors, his first steps had touched marble. Alexander had never known he was different. He accepted his life as normal—even deserved.

Having grown up surrounded by the best life had to offer, Alexander expected things to be a certain way. He felt that he had every right to the fine things to which he had become accustomed. As such, he also tended to be dismissive and elitist. Alexander refused to eat any fruit that was marked or bruised. He did not have any idea where grapes came from, or that a servant in a back room rinsed and picked each grape from its cluster before arranging them on a plate. He did not know the work that went into each cup of tea that he sent back to the kitchen when the temperature was not just right. He had no concept of life without his servants, who essentially dressed, fed, and cared for him as though he were still a child. It was only his due, and a mark of his greatness, that so many scurried to keep him happy.

Alexander made many demands of his servants and never once asked about them as people. In fact, he didn't even know any of their names. He would call out, "You, woman, move my bed so I may see a different view when I wake," or "You, boy, refill my tub with bathwater; this is not warm enough." Alexander never concerned himself with how hard the request would be. He just expected it to be done.

Alexander had a zoo of his own, filled with exotic animals from all over the world. The zoo housed monkeys, great cats, hundreds of birds, and an elephant. Each had been Alexander's favorite in turn, but now the only person they ever saw was the caretaker charged with feeding. The elephant had been prized as a baby; now he sat in a cramped enclosure, neglected and all but abandoned. The tiger was now old, toothless, and ignored by Alexander, who preferred younger and flashier animals. The monkeys had been house pets at one time, until Alexander tired of the hide and seek game he himself had taught them. They liked to hide things—shiny things—and Alexander had no patience with that trick when it was his own possessions that were missing. Though it had been hilarious when they hid his father's things.

Before it became clear that the monkeys were hiding his most prized possessions, Alexander had been convinced that it was his servant girl stealing. The girl had been fired on Alexander's calm decision, and she had left the palace begging and crying. The monkeys were banished to Alexander's zoo, losing all house privileges. Some time after she left, Alexander lost his favorite ring, but not once was the servant girl mentioned. Most of the other servants knew better than to call attention to themselves in this manner.

One young servant had managed the courage to ask for a favor once. After watching Alexander trade out his pets like clothes or jewelry, the young boy had asked to care for an animal. Alexander couldn't even remember what it was now, perhaps a dog. The event had so incensed Alexander that the boy had been removed from his job at the palace. Not that Alexander had kept the dog. It was just that the dog had been his, and a simple servant did not deserve to own something that had once belonged to a prince.

The young prince rarely left the palace. The kingdom, in his eyes, was a dirty and smelly place filled with drab people who often begged him for food. It irritated him every time his father stopped to offer assistance to those on the streets. In such cases, Alexander sulked in the corner of the palanquin, rolling his eyes and sighing dramatically. Far from noticing his father's kindness in such situations, Alexander was irritated to be stopped in the hot street, surrounded on all sides by dirty people. He had seen very little of the lives of those outside the palace. He really only saw how people affected him. He did like the stares that he received as he traveled in luxury down the road, but he never once saw the glitter of hatred saved for him after his father swept past.

The king had known his son was spoiled but had only recently seen the true extent of his son's self-indulgence. The truth was that Alexander was worse than spoiled. He was self-centered and often cruel, though it was more through thoughtlessness than genuinely cruel intent. The king had watched Alexander's situation for some years now, knowing that he needed to do something, but never quite finding the right time. He had only ever wanted the best for his son. He wanted to ensure that Alexander never went without anything, remembering the days of his own father's rule. But the king was beginning to think he had let the situation go too far, and had now waited too long to intervene. Someday, Alexander would have to take his place as king, and he worried about what kind of king his son would be.

Although the king tried to model the behavior that he wanted Alexander to learn, the boy didn't seem to pay attention. Alexander didn't care if his servants disliked him, so it never occurred to him to use kind words or to hold his temper. The king watched his son complain about the sun's heat when his servants were not quick enough to shade him. He watched as his son picked over a plate of stunning food, sending dish after dish back to the kitchen, berating those who hadn't even had a hand in its creation. He observed all these things and knew that his son would grow into the kind of man who would become a cruel and terrible king. All the while, as days and months passed, the king worried. His son was not ready to be king, and he was running out of time.

On the approach of Alexander's eighteenth birthday, the king called his closest advisor to discuss the issue. "My son's eighteenth birthday is in a matter of days, and I think the time has come to prepare him to be a better king."

The king's advisor was aware of Alexander's poor attitude and his current inability to become king, as was most of the kingdom. It wasn't something easily discussed, as he knew the king loved his son. Alexander was known to be a spoiled, pampered prince. The advisor had just the right solution.

"I have a very special gift in mind," the advisor said knowingly.

"I trust you above all others, but I don't understand how giving him more gifts will help." Giving him more seemed to be the source of the problem, rather than the solution.

"Ah, but this gift is different. What I have in mind is a certain carpet that you might remember." The two exchanged glances.

The king smiled. "I think that might be perfect."

Over the next two days, the king observed his son closely. He tried to see the man Alexander could be, struggled to envision a king amid all the selfishness and petty complaints. He yearned for a small spark of compassion, some sign that it was possible for Alexander to overcome the nature he showed now. The afternoon before Alexander's birthday, the king watched as his son strolled through the garden. After having dismissed all the servants in an angry fit, Alexander stopped to watch his birds. The king hadn't even known that Alexander spent any time with his animals. His past pets were all banished at this point to the palace zoo. He watched as his son opened the door to the cage and reached inside. He picked up something and put it back into the nests at the top, and the king realized what he was seeing. This was the spark he had hoped for, some sign that Alexander had compassion for a life other than his own. The old king smiled. He now knew that Alexander could understand the lessons he needed to learn, if only he would take the journey.

On the morning of Alexander's birthday, the king supervised all the preparations. The palace was decorated from ceiling to floor, every last marble column, in anticipation of that evening's celebration. Tonight the prince would leave his childhood behind and begin his adult life. Unlike Alexander's other birthdays, this year the king planned to give his son only one present. He was more excited about giving this one gift than all the other gifts he'd ever given his son combined.

Alexander, however, was already irritable. When he woke, his shoes weren't where he thought he'd left them, and he had almost had to walk across the cold marble to retrieve them. Fortunately, a servant showed up before he was forced to undergo that demeaning task. That didn't change the verbal tirade Alexander unleashed on the poor man. The servant rushed to do Alexander's bidding, trying to appease the young prince, only to meet more verbal abuse with the completion of each task.

As this was a very important day, Alexander chose his clothing carefully. Servants brought him robe after robe, which he rejected one by one, never without a scathing comment to the unlucky servant who happened to be carrying it at the time. Many of the robes he decided he hated so much that he tasked the servants to burn them immediately. The young servant chosen for the task complied out of fear that he might discover otherwise, but they cringed as they watched fine fabric, the gold thread and ornamentation, devoured by the flames. One of those robes could have fed his family for a month.

Alexander finally chose an intensely red outfit that he was sure would be the center of attention. By the time he was dressed, the evening's festivities had begun, and Alexander wasn't in the mood to play nice. He was relying on his birthday gifts to lift his mood.

Alexander complained through each course of the lavish dinner, although he ate more than anyone else at the table. He complained loudly about each entertainment act. The belly dancer had too much belly. The swords on the sword eater should have been called daggers. The fire breathers had bad breath. Nothing met Alexander's expectations. He hoped that his father's gifts this year would make everything better, and he fully anticipated the greatest gifts he had ever received.

Every year, Alexander was showered with gifts, each more ostentatious than the last. He couldn't wait for the gold, the fine silks and furs, perhaps a few new pets. He had been thinking of replacing his birdcages, birds and all, with something different. *Maybe I will get a new golden birdcage*, he thought. *I could fill it entirely with red birds*. When his father stood to make the presentation, Alexander's eyes sparkled with genuine excitement.

The king gestured to a servant standing in the doorway. Behind the servant stood the advisor, smiling to himself. The servant hurried, smiling, toward the group assembled around Alexander and the king. He was carrying a bundle of some kind, laid across both of his outstretched arms. Alexander couldn't understand why they all liked his father so much. Alexander's own servants seemed very sullen. They never smiled at him the way they smiled at his father. His father's voice called Alexander's attention back to the gift presentation.

"Alexander, this is your eighteenth birthday, a very important time in any boy's life, but especially in a prince's. So, today, I have a very special gift for you. Far different from any gift you have been given before."

Alexander didn't miss the fact that his father had said *a* present—as in *one*. Surely this was only the beginning of what he had in store. With slight suspicion in his eyes, Alexander stood to receive the gift.

"My son, this gift was also given to me when I turned eighteen. I hope that you enjoy it as much as I did." The king took the bundle from the waiting servant, with a softly spoken word of thanks. He unwrapped it and extended the strange gift to Alexander. Alexander took it, even more suspicious now. Whatever it was, it wasn't even new. He unrolled it. What he saw was an old, dirty carpet. It was well-worn, and he didn't doubt at all that this carpet had been his father's so many years ago. It looked ancient.

Alexander looked up at his father now, confused and irritated. "I don't understand."

The king did his best to not appear amused at his son's reaction. Gently, he said, "That gift is more special than you know. It is the most precious thing I have ever given you."

"What I know is that it's old," Alexander snapped, as he looked at the carpet with disdain. What he saw was dirt and age. *This isn't even antique*, he thought as a scowl spread across his face. *It isn't beautiful enough to be worth anything*.

"Now, Alexander, you should always do your best to show gratitude for gifts," his father gently reminded him. The king was worried, but he had expected this reaction. He knew that the prince's reaction was worse because of the audience, so he tried to handle the situation quietly.

Alexander wasn't feeling gratitude, and he hated to be corrected in front of his servants. But he did try and swallowed his reaction in anticipation of the gifts to come. Surely this was simply the first, some ceremonial thing he had to endure in order to get to the better gifts later. *Breathe*, he told himself. *Smile and wait*.

"Thank you, Father," Alexander choked out and waited. Still holding the carpet, he tilted his chin as he looked at his father. The whole room was watching now, silent, a fact that pricked at Alexander's pride. *It doesn't matter*, he told himself. *The next gift will be worth it*.

His father opened his arms wide and took the deep breath that meant he was going to speak to the entire room. "Let the celebration continue! Happy birthday to my son!"

The room echoed, "Happy birthday to Alexander," but their echo sounded a bit less exuberant than the king's. Alexander was stunned. Where were the real presents? Where were the silks and the furs and the jeweled goblets? He had been hoping for something exotic, something completely original that no one else could say they owned. The *one* thing he had gotten was an extremely old and dirty carpet.

While the rest of the guests began to eat again and enjoy themselves, Alexander stood up with his carpet in hand. He glared at his father, who watched him still from his center place at the table. Though his father's eyes were mild, Alexander was the first to look away. As Alexander stalked from the room, the celebratory noise never ceased. To his fury, he even thought that the festivity actually increased in his absence. The thought that those people were glad that he was gone lit fires in his heart. This was his birthday; if he wasn't enjoying it, it didn't seem fair that anyone else should.

Alexander went straight back to his rooms. He threw the carpet into the corner as he entered and stared out the window. His eighteenth birthday was meant to be something special, a birthday that put all others to shame. This was the birthday that marked Alexander as a man, and he felt the shame deeply. Why had his father embarrassed him like this? Was he trying to make some kind of point? Teach some kind of lesson? Alexander didn't care, and he never once glanced at the carpet as he threw himself onto the bed to ignore the world for the night. He angrily dismissed all his servants and stared into the darkness, alone. It was hours before he fell asleep.

For several days after his birthday, Alexander moped. He yelled at his servants if they bothered to get in his way. He refused to leave his quarters and spent hours wallowing in self-pity. The carpet still lay in the corner where he had thrown it. He had asked his servants to have it removed. Although they did not argue with him, they also refused to follow that direction. He broke things in his anger, and swore that, when he was king, his son would always have anything he wanted.

In the middle of the night, shortly after Alexander had finally fallen asleep, a man came to wake the prince. The boy's immediate response was anger at being awakened this way, but his mood changed when he saw who had disturbed him. This was his father's advisor, and his face was ashen with concern.

"It's your father; you need to come with me now."

Alexander ran to his father's room and knelt by the bed. "Father? What's wrong?" His father lay in the bed, propped on pillows and pale as newly fallen snow. Alexander sat gingerly on the edge of the bed and reached for his father's hand. His father wasn't able to say much, but he patted Alexander's hand in response.

The advisor stood at the end of the bed, the gravity of the situation evident to everyone present. His voice was soft and anything but gentle as he said, "Alexander, you need to ready yourself to take your father's place during this illness."

Alexander nodded. He had dreamt of inheriting his father's kingdom one day, but he hadn't wanted it to be like this. Fear and apprehension gripped his heart as he thought about what it would be like to try and fill his father's shoes. Everyone loved Alexander's father, and he seemed to be able to get anyone to do anything he wanted. Alexander knew that was not the case with him. Everyone seemed to endure his requests for his father's sake, but, if something happened to the king, how would Alexander ever be able to rule?

He left his father's room to spend hours with the advisor and several other men whose guidance he now urgently needed. Much later, as the stars twinkled out in the morning light, Alexander stepped back into his own bedroom. His eyes were drawn now to the carpet abandoned in the corner. He crossed the room, weary to his bones, and unrolled it on the floor. With the sudden onset of his father's illness, he treasured this gift that he hoped would not be the last his father was able to give.

Alexander settled onto the carpet to sit and think, hoping that it somehow held some of his father's wisdom, which he so desperately needed now. When he sat down, the most amazing thing happened. The carpet started to move. He tried to scramble to his feet, but it was too late. The carpet rippled under his feet, and rose into the air. Before he could react, the carpet swooped out the window. Alexander sat back down in shock. As he looked behind him, he saw the palace that he loved fading quickly in the distance.

The carpet bucked and swept from side to side, going far higher than Alexander was comfortable with. He hardly had the courage to look down as the earth passed underneath him. The carpet flew incredibly fast, and soon everything he recognized was gone. This was no great feat, as Alexander had so rarely been outside of the palace grounds. But the countryside that he saw now was very unfamiliar. The carpet slowed, and Alexander looked down.

Alexander saw villages, the poorest he had ever seen. The people wore tattered clothing and lived a life completely unfamiliar to him. He saw the most exotic animals: giraffes, elephants, zebras. Many of these animals Alexander had only previously seen as fine skins that he used to decorate his rooms. He cringed now at the thought, seeing the beauty they had in the wild. Then Alexander saw houses, unlike any he had ever seen in his own kingdom. Rather than walls and a roof, he saw pieces of things scrapped together to resemble houses. He couldn't help but wonder how people lived in such houses. In these villages, Alexander saw people so thin that he didn't know how they were even alive. Where was the food? The clothing? The nice houses? Alexander, for the first time in his life, truly saw poverty. "What is this place?" Alexander wondered to himself.

A voice whispered, "*Africa*."

The strange voice startled him, and Alexander eyes were even wider. "What are you that you can speak to me?"

"A friend, Alexander. You wanted a very special gift, so you should pay attention. You will not get this opportunity twice."

He didn't like it when people spoke to him this way, but Alexander was more than a little embarrassed to be reminded of his birthday. Though he was a bit afraid to say more, Alexander had to say, "I have so much, and they have so little. It doesn't seem fair."

"Alexander, you were given much so that you could help others."

Further embarrassed, Alexander realized that this had never occurred to him. He thought back on the clothes he had had burned on his birthday, simply out of his bad mood. He knew that his servants could have benefited from what he had simply wasted. He was also aware that he had indulged his petty whims his entire life, never dreaming that someone else went without.

The voice was silent for a while, as though waiting for Alexander to do something, say something. Finally, the voice whispered, "You can help these people build communities and feed their children. You can send people to teach them new ways to care for their crops and animals. You can watch this community grow."

"These people don't live in my kingdom." It had occurred to Alexander that the voice sounded a great deal like his father's oldest advisor. While he was worried about these people, he didn't want to let on that he was, so he clamped his lips together and looked away from the scene below. The voice made the sound of something like a sigh, and the carpet began to move again.

From below, something caught Alexander's eye. He looked down to see group of thin children chasing each other in the sun-baked dirt. "How can they possibly be happy, here?"

"You don't have to be wealthy to be happy, Alexander. They have a wealth inside that you don't. Look again."

Despite the abject poverty that he saw, Alexander also saw generosity—a woman helping an old widow and a man ministering to the ill. He saw families working together for the community to improve the houses and road. He watched as what little food they had was shared. Even in this place, Alexander witnessed happiness. He watched the children play though it hurt his heart to think they'd never known wealth or comfort. He saw parents who loved those children, though their hearts often hurt because their children went without. He saw people come to the village from other places.

"Who are those people?" He asked.

"People who do want to help. They have that same inner wealth, Alexander. But they have a wealth of riches too, and they choose to use it to help others. Even if these people are not *their* people, they are still people." The carpet lifted and sped away, this time leaving the village far behind them.

Lesson One:

THE VALUE OF INNER WEALTH

*A man's true wealth is the good
he does in this world.*

– Mohammed

*The gifts of caring, attention, affection,
appreciation, and love are some of the most
precious gifts you can give, and they
don't cost you anything.*

– Deepak Chopra

*Make me appreciative of the dignity of my
high vocation, and its many responsibilities.
Never permit me to disgrace it
by giving way to coldness,
unkindness, or impatience.*

– Mother Teresa

The carpet flew so fast now that Alexander could barely see what lay below them. The wind had knocked most of the dirt away from the threads now, and the carpet gleamed red and gold. Alexander covered his eyes from the force of the wind, until the carpet slowed. Below him, he saw great wet fields with standing water. They didn't look like crop fields that he knew. The land here was a great deal greener than anything he had seen before. A great wall sped underneath them, longer than any he had seen in his life. The wall ran for miles and miles, over hills and valleys, snaking back and forth for as far as Alexander could see. Ornate temples and statues of dragons had Alexander gasping in wonder, even as his eyes streamed in the ruthless wind.

When the carpet veered away from the countryside toward a city, Alexander's eyes grew even wider. He had never seen so many people in one place. Outside the dwellings here, he puzzled over what seemed to be abandoned shoes, unaware of the customs of any of the countries through which he traveled. He saw a group of people, accepting gifts of more food than they could ever eat and storing it in a building. Alexander watched the people scurry back and forth, carrying boxes and boxes of food items back to their building. He couldn't imagine how much food might be inside. *What is this*, he wondered.

"This is what it looks like when people help others in need. These people are gathering food from those who have more than they need in order to give it to those who don't have enough." Alexander watched them for a while longer, curious not only about the people who were storing the food, but about all the people he watched bringing food. Some didn't bring much at all, and some brought a great deal of food. *It is possible*, he thought, *that they were buying food specifically to bring here*. The thought seemed strange.

"Is it so strange to want to help others?" The voice was so familiar to him, and Alexander was almost positive that this was the advisor who had spent hours with him just the night before. The man had always intimidated Alexander, although he was soft-spoken. He was wise without being arrogant, as several other advisors were. Alexander knew that his father trusted this man's advice above any other. He tried to reconcile the strange journey with his desire to trust the man his father trusted.

Looking down from the gleaming carpet, Alexander saw a man sweating with work and strain in the fields. He seemed to be exhausted, but still he did not stop. The man looked tired, but he also looked content. "Why does he work so hard?"

"It is his life's work, and he would gladly work hard and suffer so that others can eat," the advisor's voice replied.

Alexander thought back on the lavish birthday celebration with embarrassment. He knew that quite a bit of food had surely gone uneaten that night. For the first time, Alexander wondered what had happened to the waste. "What is this place?"

"This is *China*. That man has lived a long and fulfilled life. This act gives him much joy, and everyone respects and loves him for his selflessness."

Alexander watched the people closely. They smiled the same smile that his father's servants did. It was one of gratefulness and love. He'd always seen the king help those around him, and this was the reward. The king never demanded respect: he'd earned it by his actions. Alexander felt bad for simply watching. "Can we help him load the food?"

The voice did not respond, but the carpet slowed down, out of the man's view, and Alexander stepped off nervously. He didn't want the carpet to race off without him, but he had the feeling that leaving him wasn't the point. He couldn't talk to the man, but Alexander pointed to the boxes and went to lift one. He had thought it would be easy, but, because he had never done anything really physical, the job was much harder than he had anticipated. He didn't want to complain to this man who had worked far longer than he had, so he bit his tongue and kept lifting.

After the pair had substantially reduced the workload, Alexander waved to the man. He made his way back to the carpet, which was still there waiting for him. He was tired and sweaty, even in these early hours, but he felt good. The carpet rose and sped up once again. Alexander covered his eyes, but he could still see the scene in his mind.

Lesson Two:

A MEANINGFUL LIFE

To do the useful thing, to say the courageous thing, to contemplate the beautiful thing: that is enough for one man's life.

– T.S. Eliot

I think the great livers, the people who are fully self-actualizing and alive, are the great givers.

– Mark Victor Hansen

Let us not say, 'Every man is the architect of his own fortune'; but let us say, 'Every man is the architect of his own character.'

– George D. Boardman

This time, when the carpet slowed, Alexander was ready. It was full daylight, and he wanted to see everything. By this time, Alexander and the carpet had covered a great deal of ground, and he had seen many people in many different circumstances.

One observation that impressed itself upon Alexander was that many of the poorest of the poor were women. He had many female servants, and he didn't even know some of their names. Now, through his travels, Alexander had seen many unjust and horrible things. He was shocked by how many of the women were mistreated or cast aside. They walked with their heads down, their eyes focused on the ground instead of on those around them. As he saw how many there were, and how important the women were to their societies, he was even more shocked by the widespread treatment.

As the carpet continued its flight, he saw a country of wide variety. This place was like nothing he had ever seen. The earth was red and dry, and Alexander saw a great table rock rising in the distance like a mountain island. He saw strange creatures, such as he had never seen in his little zoo. There was an animal that the voice told him was a *kangaroo*, as well as another creature called a *koala*. Alexander was amazed. At every turn, he saw something new. A small number of the women here had unusual tattoos on their chins. Alexander had never seen anything like it. His reaction was curiosity, unlike the disrespectful and belittling attitude he would have shown even the day before.

After a while, the carpet slowed to allow him to see a project involving a whole community that reached out to educate many women. He saw the native women talking with a woman who looked like she was from another part of the world. She was encouraging the women to have choices in their lives. She said choices and education gave women power. Alexander began to understand the great miracle of showing others how to improve their lives and how to cherish each moment of life. These women held their families and communities together and contributed a great deal to the uniqueness of their society. The people teaching the women of this place also recognized the value that these women had in their communities. He could see that their goal was to give the women back their power and their lives.

The carpet let him off to walk around a bit. He wasn't sure how he could help, but he wandered around, offering a wave and smile to anyone he saw. He finally found a woman who had just been given a pair of goats by the organization he had seen earlier. She needed a place to keep them, and she was trying to build a pen by herself. It took several hours, but Alexander stayed to help her build the pen. Even though he didn't have the words to understand her, he did understand the look in her eyes and the slight shine of tears as she tried to thank him for his help.

How often had he offered even a word of encouragement to someone who needed it? *Never.* Alexander thought back on the red robe he had worn on the night of his birthday celebration. He'd wanted for all eyes to focus on him, to look at him—why? He had everything. These women had nothing. Alexander began to see a bigger picture, where before his life view had been so small. There was so much he did not know. He was embarrassed by how much of his life he had thrown away in frivolous pursuits. Watching these women, he felt a great deal of respect for them now, and a desire to earn that same respect for himself.

The world seemed so large, with islands and continents of all kinds and people of all colors, shapes, and sizes, and Alexander led such a small and meaningless life. He resolved that he would seize every opportunity to encourage someone else and to tell others how grateful he was for all they did. The carpet increased its speed as Alexander made his plans.

Lesson Three:

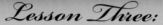

THE MIRACLE OF THE MOMENT

The purpose of life is to live it, to taste experience to the utmost, to reach out eagerly and without fear for newer and richer experience.

– Eleanor Roosevelt

We must use time wisely and forever realize that the time is always ripe to do right.

– Nelson Mandela

Miracles never cease to amaze me. I expect them, but their consistent arrival is always delightful to experience.

– **Mark Victor Hansen**

Now, Alexander wasn't covering his eyes. He didn't want to miss a moment. He was adjusting to the speed so that even through the blur he could learn something. As the carpet slowed, Alexander looked for people instead of simply seeing the landscape. The carpet had taught him great lessons thus far, and he was eager to learn the next one.

Beneath him, he saw lush tropical forests and long sandy beaches, as well as great snowcapped mountains. Where he first saw the exotic beauty of this place, green and teeming with life, now there was a sprawling city. He saw a building of the greatest beauty, positioned behind a long waterway with a mirrorlike reflection. The twin beauty he saw reflected there was enough to bring his heart into his throat. But Alexander was beginning to understand that all the beauty he had seen in each country was balanced by the darkness of poverty and disease. He wanted to do what he could to make it possible for the beauty to shine untarnished. He wanted for his father to see these wonderful places. That small part of him that was steadily growing in awareness wanted to change what he could so that the beauty was even more evident.

Here, Alexander also saw an abundance of children in the streets, some working, some begging, some sick. His immediate desire to help was tempered by fear. *I wish I could help, but there are so many! What could I possibly do to help so many?* The wealth he had always felt was infinite was beginning to feel smaller and smaller in his mind.

The voice whispered, "You do what you can. These children face overwhelming obstacles, but they manage to change their lives every day. Those people you see helping, despite the challenges presented, those people are Givers." Alexander wanted to be a Giver too. Giving felt good and right. It was so easy to make the lives of others better. Yet how difficult had he made the lives of others?

He wasn't sure how he could help here, until he saw the child a few streets away. This child was begging on a street corner, unaware of the help that was so close. Alexander could tell that this child hadn't eaten in a few days and hadn't had a good meal in much longer. The carpet brought him closer, and Alexander jumped off. He walked to the child, afraid of scaring him. The young one had his hand out, toward a man he had no idea was a prince, hoping for a few coins. When Alexander took his hand, shock touched the child's features. He hadn't known a sympathetic touch in his years on the street, and few even offered once they saw the filthy, possibly diseased, person before them. He had been happy to accept what coins he could, but nothing can substitute for the caring touch of a human hand.

Alexander took his hand and raised him to his feet. They walked together, slowly, through the several streets it took to reach the center Alexander had seen from above. He couldn't wait to see the child's eyes. He wished he could stay to see how it would turn out. When they reached the building, Alexander pointed to it and gestured to indicate that he should go inside. The child was suspicious and unsure, until a woman came out to greet him. She was angelic, even to Alexander's eyes. The woman scooped the child into her arms and took him inside, offering a small bow of her head in thanks to Alexander. He was warmed by the encounter, but he really wanted to do more. Perhaps he could help this center with its overwhelming problems after he was home again.

Alexander thought back to his countless tantrums and unreasonable demands. He'd never thought where his food came from or marveled at how wonderful it was. He had been ungrateful for the wonderful and fine gifts his father had given him. No matter how hard people tried to please him, he had never been satisfied, and he had never had a good reason. It had never made him feel better to yell at people and find fault; in fact, it made him feel worse.

Alexander looked at the people below. These people conquered immense challenges every day, and all he had done his whole life was complain. He'd never had to conquer anything, and now he felt ashamed. From these children, and the people helping them, Alexander learned that one of the rewards of being a Giver was the ability to conquer challenges, to be a champion of causes. Yes. He would champion these people and learn how to serve with passion and vigor. The day was aging, and the carpet wasted no time. They sped up again, but, this time, Alexander was watching behind him, his mind still on the children he had seen. "You didn't tell me where we were."

The voice whispered, "A place known as *India*." As they sped away, Alexander knew that the advisor was the only man who could possibly know so much as this. He doubted that even his father had seen so much of the world.

Lesson Four:

CONQUERING CHALLENGES

*I learned that courage was not the absence
of fear, but the triumph over it. The brave
man is not he who does not feel afraid,
but he who conquers that fear.*

– Nelson Mandela

*Although the world is full of suffering,
it is full also of the overcoming of it.*

– Helen Keller

*When obstacles arise, you change your
direction to reach your goal; you do not
change your decision to get there.*

– Zig Ziglar

When the carpet slowed again, Alexander was confused. The people here were dressed in the finest of clothing, and Alexander began to see wealth that even he had never dreamed possible. The carpet flew low, slower now, so that Alexander could look in through windows and listen to people's conversations. He saw a woman trying on shoes, telling the merchant that she loved that pair so much she wanted twenty pairs, one in each color. He heard a man, who had to have been a king of some kind if his wealth was any evidence, arguing with another about a deal of some kind. He was buying three houses, and, from what Alexander saw of the size of those houses, they had to have been castles. Just one of the three was larger than the finest Alexander had ever seen.

As the carpet continued its flight, Alexander saw businesses. He was awed by their size and magnificence. When he saw what they were selling, he was even further overwhelmed. These were the markets that sold the fabulous gems he had so admired. He saw glittering diamonds, gold, and jewels of magnificent splendor. As he watched the vendors trade their jewels, some of the merchants turned away from the salesmen and closed their doors. They were rejecting the diamonds offered for sale.

Alexander was stunned. "Why will they not sell the diamonds? They are more beautiful than anything I have ever seen."

With no answer, the carpet whisked him away to a jungle with deep pits of mud and dark-skinned workers slaving in the heat. Alexander watched them with horror. The advisor's voice said, "Those diamonds were bought at the cost of lives." A group of armed men ran through a neighboring village, searching out those who refused to work in the diamond mines. One man's hand was cut off, another lost his leg. Yet another was killed. He had no idea that human lives were lost so he could wear the jewelry he had so cherished.

The voice whispered, "The merchants, though they are far removed from this place, know the story behind how the gems are collected. They know about the violence behind the mining and purchase. This is why they have refused to purchase the diamonds that you admired, in order to dissuade those who take advantage of such situations. They will purchase from those who can guarantee no abuse."

Alexander was stricken with remorse. He felt sure that all his finery held a violent history, and he knew that he had to somehow fix his part in the matter. It had never even occurred to him to ask where his gems had come from or how they had been obtained. He felt odd that the finery he wore everyday might carry such guilt and resolved to remedy the situation as soon as possible. *Perhaps I can sell the jewels*, he thought. The thought was distasteful, until he remembered that the money could be used to help some of the people he had seen along this journey.

He said, "These merchants, they must be great leaders to be able to turn away such business. They know what is right, and they do it. They could make more money, but they choose to do what is right. They choose. A great leader knows how to choose."

Alexander would be a great leader. He would learn to choose. He leaned forward now, nodding to himself, as the carpet sped forward.

Lesson Five:

LEADERSHIP

*Outstanding people have
one thing in common: an absolute
sense of mission.*

– Zig Ziglar

A leader is a dealer in hope.

– Napoleon Bonaparte

*Do not go where the path
may lead, go instead where there
is no path and leave a trail.*

– Emerson

When the carpet slowed again, Alexander recognized the area a bit more than the rest. It looked more like home, even though he had never been here before. More familiar with the people in this area, he looked forward to what the carpet would show him here. They crossed wide expanses of sand, dotted with oases, until the carpet slowed at the community chosen for Alexander to observe.

What he saw here were people he had grown up thinking were too different from his own people, too different to exist in peace. The few women he could see went about with their heads covered and most of their faces. Alexander was uncomfortable at first. He wasn't sure if these were people that he wanted to help. While the thought wouldn't have bothered him at all before, now Alexander felt a twinge that could only be his conscience. He knew that somewhere in the sands beneath there were people with needs that he could help meet. There were hungry children. There were women who needed help to rescue their households from poverty and disease. He knew now that these people were no different from any other, no different from himself.

Here, in this land that was so similar to his own, with his new open mind, Alexander saw a community that was bringing the two cultures together to learn to live in peace. He knew that he wanted to be a part of this effort, that his country should be a part of a peacemaking approach to working with other countries. This community taught peace and cooperation to bridge differences. Alexander thought about his own people and the benefits that this would bring to them. He had so many ideas he wanted to bring home with him now. He couldn't wait to see the benefits to both cultures that the new peace could bring.

With thoughts of home came pain. What awaited him at home was a very ill father, and the necessity of this strange trip was now apparent to Alexander. He thought he understood his father's gift with more clarity now. Alexander hung his head, shameful but resolute. He remembered the disdain he had felt, the anger, and the sense of entitlement. He had wanted the other gifts so much that he had overlooked the gift that meant more than everything else. His father had been right when he told Alexander that this gift would be special, more precious than any other.

Here, in this place that he had previously only regarded with hatred, Alexander was learning to see inside the person, to love the person and not judge their circumstance or culture. Alexander knew that, inside, he hadn't been the person he now wanted to be. He had judged people by how they looked, how they talked, and what they possessed. He had no idea that those same people were looking at his shallow life and seeing nothing but a vain and selfish little boy. With the lessons learned from observing and interacting with these people, filling his head and his heart, Alexander knew that he could change his shallow life to make a difference now.

Lesson Six:

LEAD WITH LOVE

Let us not be satisfied with just giving money. Money is not enough, money can be got, but they need your hearts to love them. So, spread your love everywhere you go.

– Mother Teresa

As the funds you will expend have come from many places in the world, so let there be no territorial, religious, or color restrictions on your benefactions, but beware of organized, professional charities with high-salaried executives and a heavy ratio of expense.

– Conrad Hilton

I don't go by the rule book ...
I lead from the heart, not the head.

– Princess Diana

The carpet moved so fast this time that Alexander could hardly tell the difference between the land and water beneath him. It was almost as though the carpet agreed with Alexander—it was time to go home. But the journey wasn't complete yet. When they slowed enough that he could see again, Alexander saw great swatches of jungle. In places, though, the jungle looked diseased, with great holes where the trees had been cut down. Alexander had expected to see poor people here, as in most of the other places the carpet had shown him. But instead, he saw the devastation and destruction caused by men. He also saw people working to protect the great forests beneath him.

"Everything you have shown me so far was about helping people. What am I to see here?"

The voice whispered, "This is another part of the legacy of mankind. This is helping people by thinking of those who will come after you. What you leave behind will have to sustain and protect your children. Only by protecting what you see in the world, will it still be there after we are gone."

Here, Alexander learned about the gift that the forests and jungles gave to people and how valuable they were to the earth's continued survival. He learned, as the people themselves were taught, how to care for animals and crops in a way that kept the earth as well as the families healthy.

Alexander had never been in a position to learn much about farming or the care of animals. His zoo, for all he knew, maintained itself. Now, he wondered who cared for his animals and whether they were healthy. Alexander listened eagerly to lessons in this lush green classroom, ready to take whatever knowledge he could home with him.

The advisor taught Alexander that the world needed to be cared for; he took the prince around this country that he called *Ecuador* to see the damage that man had done and the steps that were being taken to correct it. Alexander knew that this lesson was not simply about the legacy of the land. It was also about the lessons he had learned. These lessons must be passed on to his children and grandchildren. They must also be passed to the people in his kingdom. When the carpet began to move again, he knew exactly where they were headed this time. It was time to go home.

Lesson Seven:

LEGACY

I choose to rise up out of that storm and see that in moments of desperation, fear, and helplessness, each of us can be a rainbow of hope, doing what we can to extend ourselves in kindness and grace to one another.

– Oprah Winfrey

But history will judge you, and as the years pass, you will ultimately judge yourself, in the extent to which you have used your gifts and talents to lighten and enrich the lives of your fellow men. In your hands lies the future of your world and the fulfillment of the best qualities of your own spirit.

– Robert F. Kennedy

The carpet swiftly approached the window they had left, and Alexander jumped off before it had even stopped. The carpet came to rest just inside the window. Before Alexander left the room, he turned for a moment to look at it again. Somehow the carpet, which had been so magical and gleaming with bright colors and life, looked sad and dusty, just as it had the night his father gave it to him. That night now seemed very long ago.

Alexander knew that the gift he had been so ungrateful for was more than just *one* gift. His father's gift was more than a dirty, old carpet. The gift was even more than a magical carpet that allowed Alexander to travel all over the world. This gift was his father's legacy, and it would be his in turn. From his experiences that night, observing and interacting with people around the world, Alexander had learned seven important lessons that would make him a far better man and king. He had learned that there are things worth more than money, and he had learned how to cultivate those traits in himself. He had learned that he could attain a better, more meaningful life by giving his wealth away, rather than spending it all on himself. He had learned to experience the miracle of the moment and to cherish the unique qualities of people from other countries, rather than getting distracted by selfish desires and failing to notice what is important for the sake of others. He had learned the joy of conquering challenge, as opposed to having everything made easy. Alexander had gained leadership skills: responsibility, creativity, and appreciation for others. He had learned the value of love, in his own life as well as in the lives of others. He had also learned a new meaning for the word *legacy*. Legacy was what his father had given him, and that legacy was a life that Alexander fully intended to live. He wanted to change not only himself, but his kingdom. And starting from his own small corner, he wanted to change the world.

Alexander walked from his own room purposefully, leaving his childhood behind him as well. In the hall, on the way to his father's rooms, the prince found himself standing directly in front of the king's oldest advisor. Alexander dropped his eyes respectfully, acknowledging the older man and the wisdom that he had never respected before. The advisor did not say anything, but stepped to the side to let Alexander pass. As he continued to his father's room, Alexander felt that, that one step had perhaps been the most significant of the night.

Alexander walked resolutely to his father's room to share his discoveries, anxious about his father's condition. Morning light streamed in the windows, peaceful. Outside, Alexander could hear the doves that filled his cages in the courtyard. Funny how he had never taken the time to notice things like that before. He couldn't believe that only a few days before he had been planning to replace them all, simply for a new look. So much had changed. He stood by his father's bedside and watched his father's face light up as he related the night's events.

"That carpet you gave me ..." Alexander trailed off, not sure how to begin.

"Eventful night, I take it?" The king smiled as he leaned back on his pillows.

"Did you know? Is that what the gift was?" Alexander watched his father's eyes for an answer.

"I told you that the carpet had been my own at one time. And I too passed an eventful night. It changed my life."

Alexander smiled a bit, but his mind wandered over the places he had visited. He wanted to return. He wanted to help. He wanted to establish his kingdom with the same ideas.

"You will make a good king one day, Alexander."

"Is the carpet what made you a good king, Father?"

His father looked as if he were far away, and time passed before he answered, "At one time, I was growing up much as you were. I too was thrilled with the wealth around me. I too was distracted by all the pleasures of palace life. I should have given you the carpet years ago, but I didn't think you were ready for it. I almost missed my chance. I hope that you will share what you have learned with your own children, without waiting."

"I think you were right. I'm not sure that I would have been ready." Alexander remembered that several times he had been presented a choice: to help or to stand aside. The younger Alexander may not have been able to put aside his distaste for what he would have seen as common, dirty beggars. He knew that choosing to step off the luxurious carpet was one of the events that had made all the difference last night. Had he simply observed, he would not have learned nearly as much. He might not have changed.

Alexander was pleased at his father's recovery, but also pleased that his time to inherit the kingdom had not yet come. He needed more time to grow and learn. "Thank you for the gift, Father. I almost didn't get to tell you. I didn't understand it at first, but I do now. This gift will change me." Alexander thought that perhaps it already had.

Alexander not only felt different, but he even thought differently about those around him. He took the time to learn the names of his servants, and those relationships grew into friendships. He smiled more, and noticed that everyone around him smiled more as well. By his next birthday, Alexander had begun to take on more responsibility in the kingdom. He had begun to organize a means of finding those who needed help, distributing food and clothing. He had sparked the idea by donating a great portion of his own wardrobe. He was well traveled in his own country now, familiar with the issues that plagued his people, as well as the strengths that made them great.

In time, Alexander grew to be a wonderful king. He drew on that one gift for the rest of his life and, as once demonstrated to him, practiced the generosity that he had seen and learned. He, as well as his kingdom, practiced generous giving. They didn't stop with their own community: Alexander and his people reached out to many that they did not know. He found great joy in both his kingdom and his life. But King Alexander had no greater joy than the day he stood before his own son and presented him the gift of an old, dusty carpet.

ALEXANDER'S SEVEN KEY LIFE LESSONS

The lessons that Alexander learns are the benefits that a giving heart receives. As he experiences the stories of each of the people he meets, in each country that he visits, Alexander's heart expands to bring everyone in. By the end of the trip, Alexander is a changed man, and he goes on to lead a productive life, successful on his life's path. The same lessons are available to each of us. We can observe these gifts in our Global Givers, and how life is enriched by giving.

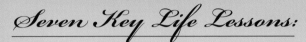

Seven Key Life Lessons:

INNER ENLIGHTENMENT

1. Inner Wealth

2. Meaningful Life

3. Miracle of the Moment

4. Conquering Challenges

5. Leadership

6. Lead with Love

7. Legacy

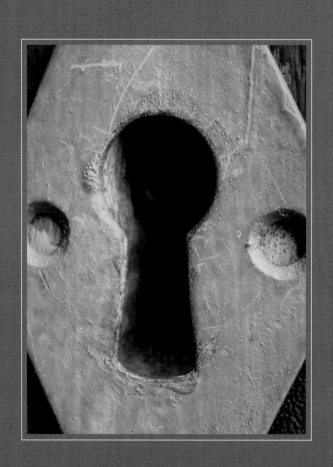

Mastering the Secret Keys

There are many people we know through either their highly successful business careers or celebrity status who are influencing, bettering, and changing our world through Global Giving.

To recognize, honor, and celebrate the Global Giving Philanthropic Legacy Leaders, we are unveiling the prestigious Luxury of Life Global Giving Hall of Fame, a designation bestowed on only one exceptional individual each year. Nominees are included in the Global Giving Business Ambassadors each year, and select Global Giving Business Partners are spotlighted who best exemplify the admirable Secret Key qualities of Global Giving.

GLOBAL GIVING
HALL OF FAME

2008 GLOBAL GIVING HALL OF FAME AWARD WINNER

Paul Newman

Paul Leonard Newman was born January 26, 1925, in Shaker Heights, Ohio and died September 26, 2008. Among his achievements as both actor and director are an Academy Award, two Golden Globe Awards, a Screen Actors Guild Award, a Cannes Film Festival Award, and an Emmy Award. But perhaps his crowning achievement has been Newman's Own, a food company which donates all profits and royalties to charity. Newman once joked that it has been an embarrassment that his salad dressing makes more money than he does. As of May 2007, the donations from Newman's Own are better than $220 million.

Newman graduated from Shaker Heights High School in 1943, and attended Kenyon College in Gambier, Ohio, to study economics. He served in the Navy during World War II, serving on the USS *Bunker Hill* as a tail gunner and radioman in the battle of Okinawa, but he was held back from the attack because of his pilot's ear infection. None of the men who were sent out on that mission from Newman's detail lived. After the war, he returned to Kenyon College to complete his degree and graduated in 1949. Later, Newman studied acting at Yale University, and then at the Actors' Studio in New York City under Lee Strasberg.

> *The only way we can give our children the best education in the world and prepare them for the next century is by funding the programs that serve them.*

Newman founded Newman's Own with writer A.E. Hotchner in 1982. They considered the experiment somewhat of a joke at first, and Newman said that having his face on the products, using his own fame to do good for others, appealed to him as "circular exploitation." They also cowrote a memoir on the subject, called *Shameless Exploitation in Pursuit of the Common Good*. Newman's giving has also funded the Hole in the Wall Gang Camps, the first of which opened in 1988 in Ashford, Connecticut. The camp, named after Butch and Sundance's gang in *Butch Cassidy and the Sundance Kid*, offers a summer residential camp to 13,000 children with life-threatening illnesses every year, free of charge, and has since expanded to include six other Hole in the Wall Camps in the United States and one each in France, Hungary, Ireland, Israel, Italy, and the United Kingdom. In 1994, Newman received the Jean Hersholt Humanitarian Award for his charity work. In 1999, he donated $250,000 for relief in Kosovo. In 2007, Newman donated $10 million to his alma mater, Kenyon College.

Newman's first major philanthropic endeavor began after his son died from a drug and alcohol overdose in 1978. Newman then helped found the Scott Newman Foundation, now the Scott Newman Center, to educate people about the dangers of drug and alcohol abuse. The foundation originally funded films and public announcements, but more recently has developed a camp for children and families affected by drug and alcohol abuse, as well as domestic violence—the Rowdy Ridge Gang Camp. Another of Newman's causes was land conservation. In 1998, he donated $500,000 to the Trust for Public Land, for the preservation of Trout Brook Valley. Newman chaired the Committee to Encourage Corporate Philanthropy, through which he sought partnerships between other philanthropists, companies with philanthropic goals, and Newman's Own.

Between 2005 and 2006, Newman began transferring his ownership in the Newman's Own food company to Newman's Own Foundation, a gift which is valued at $120 million dollars. This is in addition to the $8,746,500 in personal donations in 2006 alone. These donations went to support children, hurricane relief, education, and the arts.

I'd like to be remembered as a guy who tried—who tried to be part of his times, tried to help people communicate with one another, tried to find some decency in his own life, tried to extend himself as a human being. Someone who isn't complacent, who doesn't cop out.

www.holeinthewallcamps.org

2007 GLOBAL GIVING HALL OF FAME AWARD WINNER

Mother Teresa

Indian farmers working on a field, Sultanpur Bird Sanctuary, Haryana, India.

Agnes Gonxha Bojaxhiu was born in Albania on August 26, 1910. She joined the Sisters of Our Lady of Lareto in 1928, taking the name Sister Teresa, and performed charity work with the order in India. She founded the Missionaries of Charity in Calcutta and ministered to people stricken by poverty and illness for over forty years. She received the Nobel Peace Prize in 1979, and she was beatified six years after her September 1997 death, one step from Catholic sainthood.

*Yesterday is gone. Tomorrow has not yet come.
We have only today. Let us begin.*

Sister Teresa was already working in her calling as a nun when she received an additional call to service. She left her convent and lived among the poor in order to work directly with them. In 1950, Teresa received permission from the Vatican to start what would later become the Missionaries of Charity. Its mission was, in her words, to care for "the hungry, the naked, the homeless, the crippled, the blind, the lepers, all those people who feel unwanted, unloved, uncared for throughout society, people that have become a burden to the society and are shunned by everyone." Those who joined the order took the three traditional vows—poverty, chastity, obedience—and also a fourth: to give free service to the poor. Although it started with only thirteen members in Calcutta, the Missionaries of Charity is now a worldwide organization, with a membership of over 5,000 people.

*Being unwanted, unloved, uncared for, forgotten by everybody,
I think that is a much greater hunger, a much greater
poverty than the person who has nothing to eat.*

In 1952, Mother Teresa opened the Home for the Dying, a free hospice where the poor of any faith could receive the medical attention they needed with dignity and love during their last days. The home was renamed Kalight, or the Home of the Pure Heart. Teresa also opened a hospice for people suffering from leprosy, Shanti Nagar, or City of Peace. In 1955, she opened a home for orphaned and homeless children, Nirmala Shishu Bhavan, or the Children's Home of the Immaculate Heart. The first home outside of India was opened in 1965, in Venezuela. By the 1970s, the group had expanded around the world, with missions in Asia, Africa, the Middle East, Europe, and America.

Mother Teresa received international attention for brokering a cease-fire between Israeli and Palestinian forces to rescue thirty-seven children from a hospital at the front lines. She traveled herself to rescue these children in the war zone. She visited with Irish women in Belfast to pray for peace; in Bangladesh, she opened a home for rape victims. In the 1980s, she was able to expand into Eastern Europe, visiting people across Russia, in Chernobyl and Armenia. She convinced Fidel Castro to allow a mission into Cuba in 1986. Finally, in 1991, she returned to Albania for the first time since taking her vows, opening a Missionaries of Charity home in the capital of Tirana. In 1995, she expanded her mission into China. As of the year 2007, The Missionaries of Charity has reached over 120 countries.

God doesn't require us to succeed;
he only requires that you try.

Since her death, Mother Teresa's supporters have sought her beatification and canonization. After the shortest beatification process in modern history, she has become known as the Blessed Mother Teresa of Calcutta, the unofficial Saint of the Gutters.

People are often unreasonable, illogical, and self-centered;
Forgive them anyway.
If you are kind, People may accuse you
of selfish, ulterior motives;
Be kind anyway.
If you are successful, you will win some false
friends and some true enemies;
Succeed anyway.
If you are honest and frank, People may cheat you;
Be honest and frank anyway.
What you spend years building, someone could destroy overnight;
Build anyway.
If you find serenity and happiness,
They may be jealous;
Be happy anyway.
The good you do today, people will often forget tomorrow;
Do good anyway.
Give the world the best you have, and it may never be enough;
Give the world the best you've got anyway.
You see, in the final analysis, it is between you and God;
It was never between you and them anyway.

—Mother Teresa

2006 GLOBAL GIVING HALL OF FAME AWARD WINNER

Diana, Princess of Wales

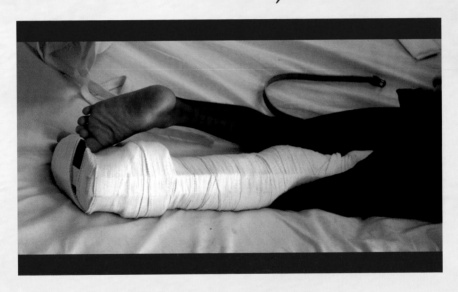

Diana Frances Spencer was born July 1, 1961. She became the Princess of Wales when she married Prince Charles of England. She was known for the elegance and beauty she brought to the royal family. She broke with tradition and ventured into philanthropic areas that were not characteristic of the monarchy. Her public divorce brought media exposure and scrutiny to Diana's life. Through that public attention, her humanitarian work received a great deal of publicity as well.

Diana worked for the Red Cross and with the International Campaign to Ban Landmines. She also worked with HIV/AIDS patients and actively raised money for AIDS foundations. She wanted people to know that the patients didn't deserve isolation, but needed hope and human kindness as well as medical attention. She didn't just give money: she spoke to people, she held their hands, and she touched their hearts.

> *I remember when I used to sit on hospital beds and hold*
> *people's hands. People used to be shocked because*
> *they'd never seen this before. To me it was quite normal.*

Diana was a patron of the Leprosy Mission, the National AIDS Trust, British AIDS Help, and Centrepoint, an organization that helps homeless youth, and was president of Great Ormond Street Hospital Children's Charity and the Royal Marsden Hospital, a hospital dedicated to cancer patients. She visited a cancer hospital in Pakistan; toured minefields; visited the minefield victims, who were often children; and traveled to Bosnia with the Landmine Survivors Network. She influenced the signing of the Ottawa Treaty, an international ban on landmines, even though she did not get to see the triumph.

Even after her death, Diana's influence is strong. The Diana Memorial Award acknowledges young people who are committed to work for change in their communities and schools, overcoming adversity. The Diana, Princess of Wales Memorial Fund was established in 1997 to continue Diana's work for the disadvantaged. It has given grants totaling over $150 million in donations since her death.

2005 GLOBAL GIVING HALL OF FAME AWARD WINNER

Audrey Hepburn

Audrey Hepburn was not just an actress: she was one of the greatest female stars of all time. And she was much more. Audrey Kathleen Ruston was born May 4, 1929, in Belgium. Though she went on to win a great many awards during her professional life—Academy, Emmy, Tony, and Grammy among them—Hepburn also served as a Goodwill Ambassador for UNICEF, an agency that works specifically for children.

*The "Third World" is a term I don't like very much,
because we're all one world. I want people to know that
the largest part of humanity is suffering.*

In 1939, her mother, then four years divorced, moved the family to the Netherlands to be safe from German attack. From 1939 to 1945, Hepburn studied ballet while at school at the Arnhem Conservatory. In 1940, the Netherlands was invaded by Germany, and Hepburn took the name Edda van Heemstra. During the occupation, she was said to have danced to help collect money for the Dutch resistance, for an audience that, of necessity, gave no applause. Hepburn lived through the German occupation and the worsening conditions after D-day in 1944. Food was scarce, and what could be found was often confiscated by the Germans for themselves. During this time, Hepburn saw her uncle and her mother's cousin shot before her eyes for their part in the Dutch Resistance. She also remembers an occasion where she saw Jewish children being loaded onto the trains for deportation.

Hepburn read Anne Frank's diary in 1946, which she said affected her very deeply. It wasn't just reading a book; it was reading her life on paper. She had been exactly the same age as Anne, and, on the exact day that Anne wrote about five hostages being shot, Hepburn's uncle was also shot.

*Taking care of children has nothing to do with politics. I think
perhaps with time, instead of there being a politicization of
humanitarian aid, there will be a humanization of politics.*

The experiences of these years are part of what led Hepburn to her involvement with the United Nations Children's Fund, or UNICEF. Her experiences had given her a unique understanding and sympathy for the plight of children around the world who were victims of war and starvation. She was appointed Goodwill Ambassador in 1988, and devoted the next few years to the poorest of children, making over fifty trips to UNICEF projects and traveling all over the world: Ethiopia, Turkey, Venezuela, Ecuador, Honduras, El Salvador, Guatemala, Sudan, Bangladesh, Vietnam, Thailand, Eritrea, Mexico, and Somalia. She worked to provide food and immunizations for orphanages, offering comfort to countless people. She used her first-hand experiences to present at Special Assemblies at the U.N., as well as to lobby on behalf of the children. In 1992, she was presented with the Presidential Medal of Freedom for her work with UNICEF, as well as the Academy Awards' Jean Hersholt Humanitarian Award, though the latter was awarded posthumously. After her death, the Audrey Hepburn Memorial Fund was created in 1993 to continue her efforts. It has raised over $1 million for various educational projects in Africa.

The enduring popularity and appeal of Audrey Hepburn can be attributed to many factors. She had a natural beauty and elegance; she has often been voted the most beautiful woman of the century. However, she also had an aura of childlike innocence which portrayed a natural charm and humor.

*There is a moral obligation that those who
have should give to those who don't.*

Time Tested Beauty Tips

For attractive lips, speak words of kindness.

For lovely eyes, seek out the good in people.

For a slim figure, share your food with the hungry.

For beautiful hair, let a child run his or her fingers through it once a day.

For poise, walk with the knowledge you'll never walk alone.

People, even more than things, have to be restored, renewed, revived,

reclaimed, and redeemed; never throw out anybody.

Remember, if you ever need a helping hand,

you'll find one at the end of your arm.

As you grow older, you will discover that you have two hands,

one for helping yourself, the other for helping others.

The beauty of a woman is not in the clothes she wears, the figure

that she carries, or the way she combs her hair. The beauty of a

woman must be seen from in her eyes, because that is the

doorway to her heart, the place where love resides.

The beauty of a woman is not in a facial mole, but true beauty in a woman is

reflected in her soul. It is the caring that she lovingly gives, the passion that

she shows, and the beauty of a woman with passing years only grows!

—Sam Levenson

(This poem has been consistently misattributed to Hepburn, as it was one of her favorites, but was actually written by Sam Levenson for his grandchild.)

2004 GLOBAL GIVING HALL OF FAME AWARD WINNER

Mahatma Gandhi

Mahatma Gandhi's final resting place.

    Mohandas Karamchand Gandhi was born October 2, 1869, and came to be known as Mahatma Gandhi, an honorific that means *great soul*. Gandhi became both a political and spiritual leader in India and led the Indian independence movement. His method was *Satyagraha*, or the nonviolent resistance to tyranny through civil disobedience. Gandhi believed that a person who served the public should lead a simple life. He had begun by renouncing the western lifestyle and clothing, wearing homespun cloth called *khadi*. He spent one day of each week in silence, believing that silence brought inner peace. He died on January 30, 1948.

Gandhi married at the age of thirteen, a prearranged marriage, and was married for nearly sixty-one years and had five children. He studied law in England and worked as a lawyer in South Africa for an Indian community struggling for civil rights. In South Africa, he faced discrimination; he was thrown off a train for refusing to move from first class to third and beaten for refusing to travel on the footboard to give room to a European traveler. He led the Indian National Congress in 1921, with campaigns for easing poverty, women's rights, religious and ethnic coexistence, ending the caste designation of Untouchable, and economic stability. Gandhi promoted and practiced a simple life, living in a self-sufficient community, wearing traditional and handmade clothing, and consuming a vegetarian diet. He undertook long fasts both for self-purification and social protest.

As the nation grew angrier and more violent against the British, Gandhi criticized both groups. He preferred the methods of noncooperation and peaceful resistance. Gandhi was arrested in 1922, found guilty of sedition, and sentenced to six years in prison, only two of which he served due to a necessary medical operation. During his absence, the Congress began to divide, and cooperation between Hindus and Muslims began to fail.

I object to violence because when it appears to do good,
the good is only temporary; the evil it does is permanent.

During World War II, Gandhi originally offered "nonviolent moral support" to the British. But after discussion with the Congress, he decided that India should not be part of a war fought for someone else's democratic freedom because India did not have that freedom for itself. "Quit India" became the demand for India's independence. Arrests and violence became increasingly common, and, on August 9, 1942, Gandhi and the entire Congress were arrested in Bombay. Gandhi was held for two years, during which time his wife died and he suffered from malaria.

Although Gandhi opposed the idea of the partition of India, he was persuaded that it was necessary to India's peaceful independence from Britain. The country was torn by violence between Muslims and Hindus, and partition was seen as a way to avoid civil war. Gandhi gave his reluctant assent, fasting in hopes of easing tensions between the two groups. He traveled to the most hostile regions, where hundreds of Hindus had been killed, raped, and forcibly converted, trying to heal the hearts of both Hindus and Muslims. He collected money to aid injured and homeless Muslims. He asked people to make amends for the wrongs that they had done.

On August 15, 1947, India was partitioned and became free. Gandhi did not attend the celebrations in the capital, instead going to Calcutta where riots still raged; but on the day that independence was granted, the riots stilled. The peace lasted until August 31. Gandhi began a fast that he said would end "only if and when sanity returns to Calcutta." People came to him and begged for forgiveness, and community leaders brought signed pledges to avoid further rioting. Gandhi broke his fast, and Calcutta kept its pledge while many other cities were lost to violence in the wake of the partition. On January 20, 1948, Gandhi was shot and killed in New Delhi by a Hindu radical.

> *You must not lose faith in humanity.*
> *Humanity is an ocean; if a few drops of the ocean*
> *are dirty, the ocean does not become dirty.*

2003 GLOBAL GIVING HALL OF FAME AWARD WINNER

Eleanor Roosevelt

Anna Eleanor Roosevelt was born on October 11, 1884, in New York City, into a high-society family and privileged life. She is well-known as a first lady of the United States. After the death of her husband, Franklin, instead of fading away, Roosevelt's prominence only continued to increase. Throughout her husband's three terms as president, Roosevelt supported the New Deal policies and worked as an advocate for civil rights.

During the 1940s, Roosevelt cofounded the Freedom House, as well as the UN Association of the United States. From 1945 to 1952, she served as a delegate to the UN General Assembly, chairing the committee behind the UN Universal Declaration of Human Rights in 1948. In 1953, she volunteered for the American Association for the United Nations.

It is not fair to ask of others what you are unwilling to do yourself.

Roosevelt is currently ninth on *Gallup's List of Widely Admired People of the 20th Century*. She was granted thirty-five honorary degrees throughout her life. The first was given by Russell Sage College in 1929 and the thirty-fifth by Clark Atlanta University in 1962. In 1968, the United Nations awarded Roosevelt the Human Rights Prize. She was also given an honorary membership into the Alpha Kappa Alpha Sorority, the only first lady to have received such an honor from the world's first and oldest African American sorority.

She resigned her membership in the American Daughters of the Revolution after their decision to ban Marian Anderson from the Constitution Hall stage in Washington DC based on a white-performers-only policy. At one point, the Ku Klux Klan placed a $25,000 bounty on her head for her protests against discrimination and racism.

In 1953, Roosevelt spent five weeks in Japan to meet with Emperor Hirohito and government ministers, as well as women's groups and those affected by the atomic bomb. In 1955, she toured Israel, Japan, Hong Kong, Manilla, Angor Wat, and Indonesia to examine the political and economic conditions of each country. At home in America, she testified before Congress in support of minimum wage. In 1962, she visited Israel for her fourth tour, to meet with the country's leaders. Roosevelt chaired the President's Commission on the Status of Women from its beginning in 1961 until her death on November 7, 1962.

2002 GLOBAL GIVING HALL OF FAME AWARD WINNER

Henry Ford

The Martha-Mary Chapel in Sudbury, Massachusetts is a nondenominational church built by Henry Ford from the many trees that were felled by the devastating 1938 hurricane.

Henry Ford founded the Ford Motor company and revolutionized both transportation and American industry through the modern assembly line and mass production. He was born on July 30, 1863, in a rural area near Detroit, Michigan. Ford worked as an apprentice machinist, servicing steam engines, and as an engineer with the Edison Illuminating Company. He was an inventor, an entrepreneur, a businessman, and a philanthropist.

*Coming together is a beginning; keeping together
is progress; working together is success.*

Early on, Ford distinguished himself from the competition by cutting the hours of the workday from nine to eight, creating the five-day, forty-hour workweek, and raising the wage from $2.34 to $5 per day. Even more than fifty years after Ford's death on April 7, 1947, his name is still included on the *Gallup's List of Widely Admired People of the 20th Century*.

In 1936, Ford created the Ford Foundation, with an initial investment of $25,000, to provide research and educational grants to develop and promote human welfare. The Foundation has since provided more than $12 billion in grants, projects, and loans. It is now America's largest foundation. Henry and his wife, Clara, contributed the funds to found the Henry Ford Hospital in 1915, which evolved into the Henry Ford Health System. During the early years of the hospital, Ford reimbursed the hospital for any yearly losses, helping to keep the doors open during the hard financial times. The Henry Ford Health System hosts an Office of Philanthropy; its mission is to provide quality care and improve lives via charitable resources in the fields of science and health care. In 2007, the Henry Ford Health System raised $72 million in charitable assets. Since the program's genesis in 1990, the Health System has received over $425 million in donations according to the Ford Health System website.

*The highest use of capital is not to make more money, but to
make money do more for the betterment of life.*

2001 GLOBAL GIVING HALL OF FAME AWARD WINNER

John D. Rockefeller

Northern Manhattan View from Rockefeller Center.

John Davison Rockefeller was born July 8, 1839, and lived until 1937. He founded the Standard Oil Company in 1870 along with several other people, including his brother William. As the oil industry grew, Rockefeller became extremely wealthy. He was the world's richest man, the first billionaire in the United States, and is often said to have been the richest person in history. The last forty years or so of his life were spent in comparative retirement, and Rockefeller began to spend money in a way that redefined modern philanthropy.

Rockefeller targeted his donations through foundations that would prove to have a substantial effect on education, as well as medical and scientific research. His foundations and personal donations were based on careful study, expert advice, and efficiency standards so that the money could have the best chance to do the most good. Several of the largest donations were given on the conditional basis that others would match his donations within a certain amount of time, guaranteeing that the university or charity in question would get all the help necessary to succeed. His foundations were instrumental in the research and ultimate elimination of yellow fever and hookworm disease. Over time, Rockefeller gave almost $250 million to the Rockefeller Foundation.

I believe it is every man's religious duty to get
all he can honestly and to give all he can.

Rockefeller provided funding for a college for African American women in Atlanta, Spelman College. He also gave sizable donations to Denison University and was instrumental in founding both the University of Chicago and Rockefeller University. Rockefeller's donations to the University of Chicago turned the small Baptist college into a true institution. The General Education Board, which he helped found in 1902, promoted education at all levels all over the United States but was especially active with black schools in the South. Other support from Rockefeller for academics found its way to Yale, Harvard, Columbia, Brown, Bryn Mawr, Wellesley, and Vassar. He supported theological schools, the Palisades Interstate Park Commission, victims of the San Francisco earthquake, the Anti-Saloon League, Rockefeller Park and other parks in Cleveland, Baptist missionary organizations, and various YMCAs and YWCAs.

With the rise of his monopoly, Standard Oil, and the ruthlessness with which he had built the company, Rockefeller had become a very unpopular public figure. Often it is that side that is remembered now, even though, by the time of his death, May 23, 1937, Rockefeller had given away about $550 million. His wealth, through his foundations and his family, continued to fund philanthropic interests throughout the twentieth century.

2000 GLOBAL GIVING HALL OF FAME AWARD WINNER

Andrew Carnegie

Andrew Carnegie was born November 25, 1835, in Dumfermline, Scotland. He immigrated to the United States with his parents in 1848 and settled in Pennsylvania. He worked a variety of jobs—bobbin boy, telegraph messenger, telegraph operator—and began investing in the Pennsylvania Railroad and other railroad-related businesses early in his career. Carnegie's father died in 1855, leaving Andrew as the sole provider for his family.

Carnegie worked his way up in the company rather quickly and became the superintendent of Pennsylvania Railroad's Western Division in 1859, at the age of twenty-six. By 1863, Carnegie was earning $42,000 per year, half of which was coming from his investments rather than his employment. Carnegie expanded his investments into the oil and steel industries, and, after the Civil War, left the railroad to focus on the ironworks. Carnegie eventually built up the Carnegie Steel Company, which he later sold to J.P. Morgan. The company was the most profitable in the world in the 1890s, and, when he sold it in 1901 for $480 million, he became the wealthiest man in the world.

There is no class so pitiably wretched as that which possesses money and nothing else.

In 1889, Carnegie published "Wealth," or "The Gospel of Wealth" as it appeared in England, in which he stated that the wealthy have a moral obligation to philanthropy. In this article, Carnegie said that the life of a wealthy person was made up of two parts: first, the accumulation of wealth, and second, the distribution of that wealth to good causes, which was the key to making that life worthwhile. Carnegie isn't the only wealthy man in history to contribute to charity, but he has been one of the first to suggest that the wealthy have a moral obligation toward philanthropy.

After this point, Carnegie spent a great deal of time and energy giving his money away, which became his occupation as much as making money had been previously. Carnegie gave the Bellevue Hospital Medical College $50,000 to found a laboratory in 1884. That medical college is now part of New York University Medical Center. In 1901, with $2 million, Carnegie established the Institute of Technology in Pittsburgh, and, in 1902, with another $2 million, he established the Carnegie

Surplus wealth is a sacred trust which its possessor is bound to administer in his lifetime for the good of the community.

Institution at Washington, DC. Carnegie also founded the Carnegie Teacher's Pension fund in 1905, with an endowment of $10 million, and then the Carnegie Corporation of New York in 1911. The Corporation was established with Carnegie's remaining $125 million, in order to aid scientific research, colleges and universities, and technical schools.

Carnegie also devoted much of his fortune to peace-related causes. In 1898, he tried to gain independence for the Philippines by offering $20 million to the United States for its recent purchase of the islands from Spain. He founded the Carnegie Hero Fund and established the Carnegie Endowment for International Peace in 1910. The Pan-American Palace in Washington, DC, was built to promote peace in the western world. His donation to the Hague Palace of Peace in the Netherlands, now the International Court of Justice, supported international arbitration to avoid war.

People who are unable to motivate themselves must be content with mediocrity, no matter how impressive their other talents.

When Carnegie died in 1919, he had established some 3,000 libraries worldwide, promoting the concept of free public libraries, and had given away over $350 million. Adjusted for inflation, that figure is approximately $4.3 billion in today's dollars.

No man can become rich without himself enriching others.

GLOBAL GIVING
HALL OF FAME
NOMINEES FOR 2009

BONO

Paul David Hewson was born May 10, 1960, in Ireland. Originally, his nickname was Bono Vox, an adaption of the Latin phrase for "good voice." As the main vocalist for the band U2, Bono writes almost all the lyrics for their songs, often with political, social, and religious themes. He states that his motivation for philanthropy came from viewing a benefit show, the Secret Policeman's Ball, as far back as 1979. With his fame and reputation in the music industry, Bono began to focus on philanthropic work in 1986. In that year, he helped organize Amnesty International's Conspiracy of Hope Tour, and he visited Ethiopia with World Vision.

I love this work I do. It's a privilege to serve the poor.

Bono has been instrumental in the creation of several charitable organizations: the ONE Campaign to "Make Poverty History;" DATA (Debt AIDS Trade Africa), which works toward the eradication of poverty and HIV/AIDS in Africa; Product Red, which works to raise money for the Global Fund to Fight AIDS, TB, and malaria; and Edun, a clothing company he started with his wife that benefits countries struggling with poverty through trade rather than financial aid. His work with DATA earned Bono a place on Forbes's Generous Celebrity List.

Celebrity is currency, so I wanted to use mine effectively.

Bono's philanthropic involvement has ranged from writing to participating in songs for a benefit. He wrote "Silver and Gold" for Steve Van Zandt's Artists Against Apartheid and participated in an additional single, "Sun City." He has visited Ethiopia, Nicaragua, and El Salvador to help children in conflict areas. In 1993, he visited Hamburg, Germany, to attend the Festival Against Racism. Bono donated $50,000 to One in Four, a charity in Ireland, for the survivors of sexual abuse. He has received three separate nominations for the Nobel Peace Prize, in 2003, 2005, and 2006. *Time* magazine ranked Bono as one of the 100 Most Influential People in both 2004 and 2006. It was in 2005 that the magazine named him as a Person of the Year, an honor shared that year with Bill and Melinda Gates. In 2007, the United Kingdom granted Bono an honorary knighthood.

When the story of these times gets written, we want it
to say that we did all we could, and it was more
than anyone could have imagined.

WARREN BUFFETT

Downtown Omaha at dawn.

Warren Edward Buffett was born August 30, 1930, in Omaha, Nebraska. He was likely to have been exposed to the stock markets early because his father was a stockbroker. As a child, Buffett worked delivering newspapers and filed his first tax return at the age of thirteen. He claimed a $35 deduction for his bicycle. Because of his entrepreneurial successes early in life, Buffett considered going straight into business rather than college studies, but his father intervened. Buffett studied at Columbia Business School under Benjamin Graham, who had a great influence on Buffett's life. In 1965, Buffett took over the textile company Berkshire Hathaway.

If you're in the luckiest 1 percent of humanity, you owe it to the rest of humanity to think about the other 99 percent.

In 2007, Buffett was listed as one of *Time* magazine's "100 Most Influential People in the World." He is considered to be one of the world's greatest stock market investors, and, with an estimated net worth of $62 billion, he is the richest person in the world as of 2008. Despite his immense wealth, he continues to live in the same city he was born, in the same home he purchased in 1958. Originally purchased for $31,500, that home is now worth more than $700,000. Buffett does not carry a cell phone or keep a computer at his desk, and he drives his own Cadillac DTS. Frugality despite his immense wealth is part of Buffett's reputation.

Someone's sitting in the shade today because someone planted a tree a long time ago.

Having said for years that his fortune would be given to philanthropic causes, but not until after his death, Buffett changed his mind in 2006 after the death of his wife, Susan Thompson. At the age of seventy-five, Buffett announced that he would gradually give away his Berkshire holdings each year to five separate foundations, the largest earmarked for the Bill and Melinda Gates Foundation. The Gates give Buffett credit for having inspired the way they think about giving. The Gates Foundation focuses on world health, fighting malaria, HIV and AIDS, and tuberculosis, as well as improving libraries and schools in the United States. Buffett's donation of 10 million Berkshire shares to this foundation, worth around $31 billion as the share value stood at the time of the announcement in 2006, is the largest charitable donation in history. He also announced his plans to donate additional stock to the Susan Thompson Buffett Foundation, as well as other foundations belonging to his three children.

The impact of Warren's generosity will not be fully understood for decades.

—Bill and Melinda Gates

Buffett serves on the board of trustees for Grinnell College and the board of directors for the Gates Foundation. Once a year, Buffett participates in an eBay auction where a person purchases the chance for a private lunch with Buffett, and the proceeds are given to charity. In 2008, that amount came to $2,110,100 and benefited the San Francisco Glide Foundation. The auction winner can bring seven people to lunch, and they can talk with Buffett about anything they like, except what he's buying and selling.

I always had the idea that philanthropy was important today,
but would be equally important in one year, ten years,
twenty years, and the future generally.

Buffett's views on money are unique, bold, and surprising. Once, he issued a challenge to fellow members of the Forbes 400, offering to donate $1 million to charity if the others would admit that they pay less of a percentage of their income in taxes than their own secretaries. Buffett does not plan to save a great deal of his fortune for his children's inheritance. He has made statements frequently about his distaste for the transfer of great fortunes from generation to generation. He plans to leave enough to his three children so that they feel "they could do anything," but not so much that they "feel like doing nothing." His opinion on the matter of massive inheritance is found in his comparison of welfare officers and food stamps to a trust officer with stocks and bonds.

It's better to hang out with people better than you ...
Pick out associates whose behavior is better than
yours and you'll drift in that direction.

BILL AND MELINDA GATES

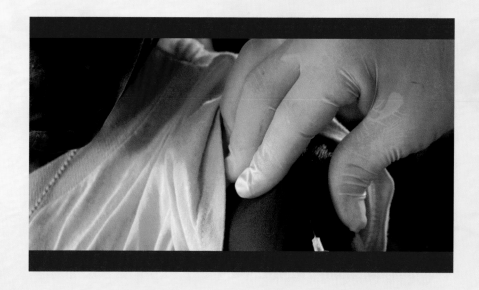

    Bill Gates was born October 28, 1955. He has worked his way through the titles of entrepreneur, CEO, chief software architect, author, and philanthropist. He established Microsoft in 1975 with his friend Paul Allen and has since been ranked first on the *Forbes* 400 from 1993 to 2007 and first on the *Forbes* list of the World's Richest People from 1995 to 2007. Melinda Gates was born on August 15, 1964. She joined Microsoft in 1987 after receiving an MBA from Duke University. The couple eventually met at a Microsoft event and were married on January 1, 1994.

Bill Gates's plan was always to engage in more philanthropy after his retirement, but his efforts began in earnest after his marriage to Melinda. In 1994, Gates created the William H. Gates Foundation, which was funded by the sale of some of his Microsoft stock. In 1995, Microsoft began to donate money and software toward outfitting public libraries with computers. In that same year, Gates published *The Road Ahead* and, in 1999, he authored *Business @ the Speed of Thought*, donating the profits from both books to nonprofit organizations. The Bill & Melinda Gates Foundation was established in 2000, combining three of the family's foundations into one. The Bill & Melinda Gates Foundation is the largest "transparently operated" private charitable foundation in the world.

> *As we look ahead into the next century,*
> *leaders will be those who empower others.*

—Bill Gates

The Bill & Melinda Gates Foundation provides funds for farming and agriculture, college scholarships for minorities, and AIDS prevention and also focuses on other diseases in third-world countries around the world. It is composed of three grant-making programs: Global Health, Global Development, and the United States Program. The foundation has pledged over $7 billion to a variety of causes, including $210 million for the Gates Cambridge Scholarships, and $1 billion to the United Negro College Fund. In 2006, a pledge from Warren Buffett doubled the size of the foundation. In 2008, Gates officially retired, announcing that he was leaving his full-time position at Microsoft for a full-time career in philanthropy.

We started our foundation because we believe we have a real opportunity to help advance equality around the world, to help make sure that, no matter where a person is born, he or she has the chance to live a healthy, productive life.

—Melinda Gates

In 2005, Bill and Melinda Gates shared the honor of *Time* magazine's Persons of the Year with Bono. *Time* also noted that Gates was one of the one hundred people who most influenced the twentieth century. In 2006, Bill and Melinda Gates were awarded the Order of the Aztec Eagle for their work in Mexico with the program *Un país de lectores* in health and education.

I realized about ten years ago that my wealth has to go back to society. A fortune, the size of which is hard to imagine, is best not passed on to one's children. It's not constructive for them.

—Bill Gates

AL GORE

Albert Arnold Gore, Jr., was born March 31, 1948. He graduated from Harvard University in 1969 with honors and a degree in government. After his graduation, Gore enlisted in the U.S. Army, serving in Vietnam as a military journalist. From 1993 to 2001, he served as the forty-fifth vice president of the United States under President Bill Clinton. He is now an environmental activist, author, and businessman. Gore served in American politics for over three decades.

No matter how hard the loss, defeat might serve as well as victory to shake the soul and let the glory out.

During his Senate years, Gore was active in environmental issues, with a particularly central role in the 1980 Superfund bill to address chemical spills and land dumps. During his vice presidency, he continued to act on environmental concerns, writing *Earth in the Balance: Healing the Global Environment* in 1992. In recent years, Gore has devoted his attention to such causes as global warming and climate change.

We, the human species, are confronting a planetary emergency—a threat to the survival of our civilization that is gathering ominous and destructive potential.

In 2004, Gore cofounded Generation Investment Management, where he serves as chair, a company that plans to create environmentally friendly investment portfolios. Gore founded and currently chairs the Alliance for Climate Protection. He is also a partner in Kleiner Perkins Caufield & Byers, a venture capital firm, where he heads the climate change solutions group. In 2006, Gore authored *An Inconvenient Truth* and starred in the documentary of the same name. In 2007, Al Gore was awarded the Nobel Peace Prize for his work with public knowledge of the environment, shared by the Intergovernmental Panel on Climate Change. He donated his half of the $1.6 million award to the Alliance for Climate Protection.

We are now in a Global Age. Like it or not, we live in an age when our destinies and the destinies of billions of people around the globe are increasingly intertwined.

ANGELINA JOLIE

Angelina Jolie Voight was born June 4, 1975, to Jon Voight and Marcheline Bertrand. Famous first for her father's career, and then for her own, Jolie is now a Goodwill Ambassador for the United Nations Refugee Agency. When asked what she does with her money, her reply was, "Save one third, live on one third, and give away one third."

My role as goodwill ambassador has made my work as a film star relatively dull. I can't find anything that interests me enough to go back to work. I'm simply not excited about anything. I'm not excited about going to a film set.

Jolie has three biological children with Brad Pitt—Shiloh, Knox, and Vivienne—and has adopted three others as well: Maddox, her first child, who was born in Cambodia; Pax, who was born in Vietnam; and Zahara, who was born in Ethiopia. Jolie became aware of the humanitarian crises worldwide while filming *Tomb Raider* in Cambodia. She began to visit refugee camps to learn more about the conditions and situations. Jolie's first field visit was in February 2001, on an eighteen-day mission to Sierra Leone and Tanzania. She returned to Cambodia, as well as visiting Pakistan where she donated $1 million for Afghan refugees. By August of 2001, the UNHCR was impressed enough by her devotion that she was named Goodwill Ambassador at the headquarters in Geneva. Throughout the next three years, Jolie visited refugee camps all over the world: Thailand, Ecuador, Namibia, Sri Lanka, and Jordan. She has been significantly involved with the refugee situation in the Sudan, visiting resulting camps in Chad, Egypt, and Kenya. Jolie also visited Pakistan in the wake of the Kashmir earthquake. In 2007, Jolie and Pitt made an additional $1 million dollar donation to three relief organizations in Chad and Darfur. That same year, she also visited Iraq and Syria for the first time, meeting with Iraqi refugees as well as U.S. troops and multinational forces.

Jolie has increased her political involvement as well, attending World Refugee Day in Washington, speaking at the World Economic Forum, and lobbying for humanitarian interests. Jolie helped found the National Center for Refugee and Immigrant Children with a donation of $500,000 in 2005, and her own Jolie-Pitt Foundation in 2006. She was the first recipient of the Citizen of the World Award by the United Nations Correspondents Association, awarded the Global Humanitarian Award by the UNA-USA, the Freedom Award by the International Rescue Committee, and citizenship in Cambodia by King Norodom Sihamoni for her conservation work there, where she has pledged $5 million toward a wildlife sanctuary.

ROBERT REDFORD

Charles Robert Redford, Jr., was born August 18, 1936, in Santa Monica, California. His career has spanned multiple professions: from businessman to model, from actor, producer, and director to environmentalist and philanthropist. He attended high school in Los Angeles at Van Nuys High, and graduated in 1954 with a baseball scholarship to the University of Colorado. Later, Redford studied painting at the Pratt Institute in Brooklyn, and also attended classes in theatrical set design at the American Academy of Dramatic Arts in New York City. Redford has three children and four grandchildren and currently resides in Sundance, Utah.

We do not own this place, we are just passengers.

As Redford's popularity grew, both as an actor and director, he used that influence to promote environmental causes. He has actively advocated environmentalist causes since the 1970s. Redford purchased property in Utah, turning it into a ranch and ski resort. In 1980, he created the Sundance Institute, which now hosts one of the most influential film festivals in the world. Redford has been a trustee on the board for the Natural Resources Defense Council for almost thirty years. In 2002, he joined the Advisory Board for the Reebok Human Rights Foundation. He is also a board member of The Gaylord A. Nelson Environmental Endowment at the Institute for Environmental Studies at the University of Wisconsin, the National Council of the Smithsonian's National Museum of the American Indian, the Environmental Policy Center, Navajo Education and Scholarship Foundation, Solar Lobby, and Yosemite Institute.

I came to a place where I realized what true value was. It wasn't money. Money is a means to achieving an end, but it's not the end.

Redford's contributions to environmental legislature have encompassed the Clean Air Act, the Energy Conservation and Production Act, and the National Energy Policy Act. He was involved in the 1975 fight against the construction of a coal-fired power plant in Southern Utah, in an area surrounded by five national parks. This area was threatened a second time by commercial expansion, and in 1997 Redford and other activists succeeded in having the area designated as the Grand Staircase-Escalante National Monument.

In 1983, Redford founded the IRM, Institute for Resource Management, which serves to unite environmentalists and industrialists for conflict resolution and the promotion of sustainable development. The IRM has addressed problems such as the future of electric power, resource development on reservation lands, offshore oil leasing, and urban air quality. Redford's final act in leadership of the IRM was the 1989 Global Warming Summit in Sundance, Utah—Greenhouse

Glasnost—which brought together leadership in the fields of industry, science, and art from the United States and the Soviet Union to raise awareness of global warming. In 1998, Redford put 860 acres of his own property in Sundance into a land trust for protection against development. He continues his work with the North Fork Preservation Alliance for the protection and responsible development of the North Fork of the Provo Canyon in Utah.

I think the environment should be put in the category of our national security. Defense of our resources is just as important as defense abroad. Otherwise what is there to defend?

Redford has received many awards relating to his environmental work: Audubon Medal Award (1989), United Nations Global 500 Award (1987), Earth Day 5 International Award (1993), Nature Conservancy Award (1994), National Medal for the Arts (1997), Freedom in Film Award (2001), Forces of Nature Lifetime Achievement Award (2004), and Kennedy Center Honors (2005).

We've poisoned the air, the water, and the land.
In our passion to control nature,
things have gone out of control.
Progress from now on has to mean something different.
We're running out of resources and
we are running out of time.

OPRAH WINFREY

Oprah Gail Winfrey was born January 29, 1954, in Kosciusko, Mississippi. Although she was born into rural poverty to unmarried parents and grew up in a dysfunctional home in an inner-city environment, Oprah transcended her beginnings and is now known as the successful host of her own internationally syndicated talk show, an Academy Award nominated actress, a media mogul in her own right, a philanthropist, and possibly the most influential woman in the world. Her talk show is the highest rated in the history of television. Winfrey began working in radio while still in high school, and worked as a coanchor on a local news show at the age of nineteen. In this position with Nashville's WLAC-TV, Winfrey was both the youngest and the first black female news anchor. Soon after, she moved into daytime talk shows, eventually launching her own production company. By the age of thirty-two, Winfrey was a millionaire.

I am a woman in process. I'm just trying like everybody else.
I try to take every conflict, every experience,
and learn from it. Life is never dull.

Winfrey has been called the world's most powerful woman by both CNN and *Time*, the most influential woman in the world by *American Spectator*, one of the most influential people of the twentieth century by *Time*, and one of *Time's* most influential people for the years 2004, 2005, 2006, 2007, and 2008. *Life* has listed Winfrey both as the most influential woman and the most influential black person of her generation, as well as America's most powerful woman. *Ladies Home Journal* ranks Winfrey as the most powerful woman in America. Winfrey, in 1998, became both the first female and the first African American to top *Entertainment Weekly's* list of the 101 most powerful people in entertainment. Winfrey was also named the most powerful celebrity in the world for the years 2005, 2007, and 2008 by *Forbes*. In 2005, a public poll ranked Winfrey ninth on a list of the greatest Americans; she was the top-ranking female on the list.

Unless you choose to do great things with it, it makes
no difference how much you are rewarded,
or how much power you have.

Winfrey's philanthropic endeavors began in 1998 with Oprah's Angel Network, which encourages people around the world to make a difference in the lives of others in need. The network has raised over $51 million, and all funds raised go to charity, as Winfrey herself covers all the administrative costs. Though her public charity and her show are known for benevolence, Winfrey donates more personally than any other show-business celebrity in America. She is listed at a rank of thirty-two on *Business Week's* list of the top fifty most generous philanthropists, with an estimated total of $303 million donated. When she asked her viewers to donate after Hurricane Katrina, she matched the $11 million raised with $10 million of her own. In 2002, Winfrey became the first person to receive the Bob Hope Humanitarian Award. In 2006, Winfrey took 1,065 people, her employees and their families, on a Hawaiian vacation to celebrate twenty years of hard work.

The more you praise and celebrate your life,
the more there is in life to celebrate.

In 2004, Winfrey and a team filmed a special in South Africa, taking a twenty-one-day trip around the country to visit schools and orphanages, and to distribute clothing, toys, and school supplies to 50,000 children. The episode garnered over $7 million in donations from viewers. Oprah opened a school near Johannesburg in 2007 with an investment of $40 million. Although Winfrey has never had children, she has stated that her students at the Oprah Winfrey Leadership Academy for Girls are her daughters. She has plans to spend a great deal of time in her retirement in a house on the campus, where she plans to live the same as the students do: the same dishes, sheets, curtains, food, et cetera.

I don't think you ever stop giving. I really don't. I think it's an
on-going process. And it's not just about being able to write
a check. It's being able to touch somebody's life.

GLOBAL GIVING
AMBASSADORS

TOM ARNOLD (IRELAND)

Abbey ruins, Tipperary County, Ireland.

Tom Arnold's experience includes time as a senior economist with ACOT, the Farm Advisory Service in Ireland; the assistant secretary general with the Irish Department of Agriculture and Food; and chief executive of Concern Worldwide, which is an international humanitarian relief organization and the largest humanitarian organization in Ireland. In 2003, Arnold was appointed to the United Nations Millennium Projects Hunger Task Force, and is also a member of the International Food Policy Research Institute. He serves as a member of the Irish Hunger Task Force, which is working toward a strategy by which Ireland can contribute to ending world hunger, and he also serves as vice-chair of the Trans Atlantic Food Aid Dialogue. In addition, Arnold has authored many articles with the theme of poverty, hunger, and aid delivery.

SHIRIN EBADI (IRAN)

Shirin Ebadi has experience as a lawyer, a human rights activist, and also as founder of the Children's Rights Support Association. In 2003, Ebadi was awarded the Nobel Peace Prize for her work with women's and children's rights. She is the first Iranian, and the first Muslim woman, to receive the Nobel Peace Prize. Since that time, she has lectured and taught a variety of courses on such topics as women and human rights. In 2006, she helped found the Nobel Women's Initiative to bring the experiences of other Nobel Peace Laureates together in the efforts of supporting women's rights around the world.

MALIZOLE GWAXULA (SOUTH AFRICA)

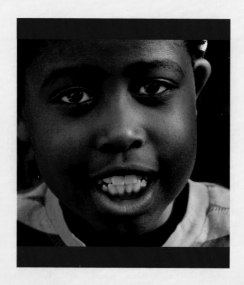

Malizole "Banks" Gwaxula has been a teacher for more than twenty years at the Emfundweni Primary School in Zwide, Port Elizabeth. He helped found the Leaderwise Schools Project to develop students' leadership skills and also helped to found the Ubuntu Education Fund, which employs more than fifty-five people in Zwide, reaching out to more than 40,000 children and families with educational and health initiatives. Long known locally for his goals of bettering the communities around him, Gwaxula is well known all over Port Elizabeth. Recently he has been recognized internationally by being included on the New Brighton Library's Hall of Fame and recognized at the World Economic Forum. He was also a finalist in the Schwab Foundation Social Entrepreneur of the Year Award in 2006.

MAMMOOTTY (INDIA)

Dawn on the Ganges.

Mammootty is a popular, award-winning actor in Malayalee Indian films. He shares the record of winning the National Film Award for Best Actor the most times with fellow actor Kamal Haasan. He has appeared in more than three hundred Malayalam movies and is considered one of the finest actors in Indian cinema. He has won three national awards, six state awards, and nine Filmfare awards for Best Actor. In 1998, the Indian government honored him with the Padma Shri, an award to recognize his contributions to Indian cinema.

Mammootty supports a variety of humanitarian causes which include the Askshaya project; the Pain and Palliative Care Society, which works with cancer patients; Kazhcha, which gives free eye care; Jeevan Jothi, which supports people seeking treatment for a wide variety of illnesses; a charity project aimed at eradicating child abuse and child labor; and by donating food to regions affected by illness and tragedy.

ADI ROCHE (IRELAND)

Adi Roche founded the Chernobyl Children's Project International and serves as the international executive director. The organization helps children and families affected by the Chernobyl disaster and has given more than $120 million in aid. Not only does the program offer pediatric surgery, community centers, medical aid, hospice, and nursing, but it also offers support through foster families for the more than 12,000 children brought to Ireland.

Roche has been given numerous awards for her work, including the European Woman Laureate Award, Irish Person of the Year, European Person of the Year, and the Medal of Francysk Skaryna given by the Belarusian government. She was the keynote speaker at the United Nations General Session on the eighteenth anniversary of the Chernobyl disaster and was appointed to represent NGOs on the Steering Committee of the United Nations' International Chernobyl Research and Information Network.

For it is in giving

that we receive.

—St. Francis of Assisi

Global Giving
Business
Ambassadors

BENTLEY

Bentley prides itself on being a socially responsible automobile manufacturer. As such, Bentley operates under an environmental policy to minimize its impact on the environment, both locally and globally. Bentley's principles are to integrate these factors into all business decisions and to comply with all relevant environmental legislation. The Crewe site is under continual improvement for environmental performance. Bentley demonstrates a strong commitment to pollution prevention and works toward the optimization and efficient use of resources and recycling opportunities. In the past decade, Bentley has reduced total energy consumption by almost 30 percent, and manufacturing process CO_2 emissions have declined more than 20 percent.

www.bentleymotors.com

CARTIER

Cartier has a wide approach to corporate responsibility. The corporate responsibility director, Pamela Caillens, makes the point that corporate responsibility is more important than philanthropy: "The latter, in other words, charity initiatives, concern the way the company chooses to spend its money. CR [corporate responsibility] exposes how the company chooses to earn it. Because you don't earn money at any cost."

Cartier's variety of causes includes environmental issues and social responsibility, as well as patronage of the arts. Cartier's environmental approach involves recycling and clean energy. In 2007, Cartier contracted with the French Electricity Board for renewable energies in each of its boutique shops. Even the labeling paper is undergoing change as Cartier works toward utilizing sustainable sources. Cartier joined the Council for Responsible Jewelry Practices in May 2005, which means that any diamond bought from Cartier is guaranteed to be free from armed conflict, war-zone smuggling, and child labor. Cartier also joined a partnership with the Women's Forum for Economy and Society, which awards $20,000 in grants and personal coaching to five female entrepreneurs each year, from specific areas of the world. Cartier also supports several children's associations: the World Childhood Foundation in Sweden and K.I.S.S. Polo in Argentina, among others.

www.cartier.com

Kindness in words creates confidence. Kindness in thinking creates profoundness. Kindness in giving creates love.

—Lao Tzu

MARRIOTT INTERNATIONAL

Marriott International serves more than 2,900 hotels in the United States and sixty-seven other countries. Ranked as one of the most admired companies in the lodging industry and one of the best places to work by *Fortune*, Marriott is also an EPA Energy Star Partner. In 2007, Marriott International announced the Youth Career Initiative to provide job opportunities for disadvantaged youth around the world through education and on-the-job training. The program offers six months of training along with on-the-job experience in the hospitality industry and is currently operating in Australia, Brazil, Poland, Romania, Thailand, Jordan, Mexico, Ethiopia, Indonesia, and the Philippines, expanding into Egypt, Costa Rica, India, Vietnam, the Caribbean, Latin America, and Southeast Asia. The J. Willard and Alice S. Marriott Foundation made a $250,000 grant to further expand the Youth Career Initiative, matched by a $250,000 challenge grant to encourage others to support the program. Also, in 2007, *Condé Nast Traveler* presented JW Marriott with the World Savers Award for corporate social responsibility.

Marriott focuses its social responsibility program as the Spirit to Serve Our Communities. The SERVE Initiative is based on Shelter and Food, Environment, Readiness for Hotel Careers, Vitality of Children, Embracing Diversity, and People with Disabilities.

www.marriott.com

www.marriott.com/corporateinfo/culture/coreValues.mi

Until he extends his circle of love to all living things,
man will not himself find peace.

—Albert Schweitzer

RITZ-CARLTON HOTELS

The Ritz-Carlton Hotel Company operates in twenty-three countries around the world with seventy hotel and resort properties; they also offer fractional residences in the United States as the Ritz-Carlton Club and employ over 32,000 people. Ritz-Carlton launched their Give Back Getaway program April 1, 2008. Seventy hotels worldwide will offer at least one volunteer opportunity for guests, including conservation and humanitarian projects. The program focuses on opportunities that will enrich lives in the community, as well as provide a meaningful experience for the hotel's guests. The Give Back Getaway experience will be unique to each destination. All profits from the program are donated to the partner organizations. The Give Back Getaway program is the most recent venture from Ritz-Carlton's social and environmental responsibility sector, Community Footprints.

http://corporate.ritzcarlton.com/en/About/GiveBackGetaways.htm
www.ritzcarltonclub.com

My father used to say, "You can spend a lot of time making money. The tough time comes when you have to give it away properly." How to give something back, that's the tough part in life.

—Lee Iacocca

STARWOOD HOTELS & RESORTS

Starwood operates over 850 properties, across more than ninety-five countries, with more than 14,500 employees. Starwood staff and associates around the world participate in volunteer and mentoring programs, such as the StarCare for the Community service program, where employees donate eight hours per year to volunteer work in their own communities. Starwood hosts local clean-up days, and volunteers build homes for local low-income families and raise charitable funds. Additionally, Starwood partners with the Special Olympics and acts as sponsor through donations, cause-related marketing, and the Starwood Preferred Guest Program.

In 2001, Starwood Hotels offered two days of volunteer activities in the Bronx school district with New York Cares. A variety of projects were scheduled at two separate schools, such as murals, outdoor play areas, and landscaping. Master chef Michel Nischan introduced middle school students to healthy nutrition. In Atlanta, at a similar City Cares Day, Starwood employees worked on three elementary school campuses, building an amphitheater and working with landscaping and murals. The Starwood Foundation sponsors City Cares, the parent organization for New York Cares Day, and is committed to servathons in New York, Atlanta, Boston, Washington DC, and Chicago.

www.starwood.com

www.starwoodhotels.com

www.citycares.org

The best philanthropy is constantly in search of the finalities—a search for a cause, an attempt to cure evils at their source.

—John D. Rockefeller

*The great aim of education is
not knowledge but action.*

—Herbert Spencer

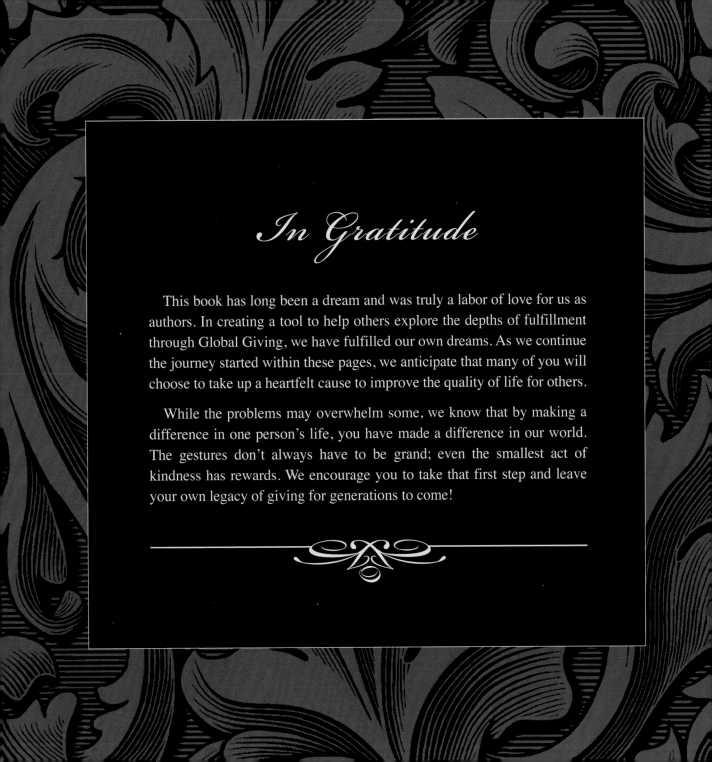

In Gratitude

This book has long been a dream and was truly a labor of love for us as authors. In creating a tool to help others explore the depths of fulfillment through Global Giving, we have fulfilled our own dreams. As we continue the journey started within these pages, we anticipate that many of you will choose to take up a heartfelt cause to improve the quality of life for others.

While the problems may overwhelm some, we know that by making a difference in one person's life, you have made a difference in our world. The gestures don't always have to be grand; even the smallest act of kindness has rewards. We encourage you to take that first step and leave your own legacy of giving for generations to come!

Acknowledgments

From Joy Macci, PhD: To my loving mother, Torrie Harris Baher, who inspired me by her works of courage, strength, and faith to help develop me into who I am today. To Jim Newton, who through his financial gifts and kindness opened the doors to international tennis and life. And to Zig Ziglar, whose life and work showed me "We can get everything we want in life, if we help enough other people get what they want."

From Alexandria Hilton, MA: To the inspiring role models who have contributed to my passion for philanthropy: my grandmother, Anna Fuchs, who demonstrated charity to others throughout her life through compassionate caregiving; my mother, Antoinette Hill, a role model of generosity who always made room at the table to feed other children in addition to her own family of ten; and my daughter, Aislinn, who focused on philanthropy as a teenager, organizing and leading several fundraising campaigns, including one to better the lives of child soldiers in Africa. And thank you to my loving husband, Dick Ferrington, who supports my dreams.

From both Joy and Alexandria: We are thankful and deeply grateful to our amazing *Enjoy: Luxury of Life* Dream Team: Dee Burks, Anna Sajecki, Daniela Savone, Lisa Crowder, Gerry Robert, and Wendy Gallagher, whose endless time, energy, expertise, and teamwork helped bring our book's divinely inspired purpose and vision into reality. Thank you!

About the Authors

MEET JOY MACCI, PHD

The lessons of Global Giving and World Wealth often arrive from unexpected events. As a young girl in Arkansas, I never really dreamed that one day I'd travel the world and reach out to others through Global Giving. I learned the value of hard work from my mother. Born the youngest child in the family, my siblings were significantly older than me. My father, a decorated World War II veteran, was in poor health and lived permanently in the Veteran's Hospital in Kansas.

I grew up watching my mother single-handedly raise her three children by herself, which was difficult, but still she found time for others and volunteered for various charitable organizations and events.

At the age of thirteen, I took up tennis and was naturally gifted, becoming ranked in both the state and region. With much hard work, I earned multiple scholarships to one of the country's top tennis camps and was one of the top eight players from the United States and Mexico to qualify for John Newcombe's International Tennis Tour Team to England and Mexico.

We spent several weeks traveling to England and Mexico (including Wimbledon and tournaments throughout the countries), as well as various locations around the United States. This opportunity was a great honor, but my family did not have the money to cover the expenses. However, one of my tennis buddies, Jim Newton, who would fly in two to three times a month to play, asked some of his wealthy friends to sponsor me and cover my expenses.

Thanks to Jim's kindness and gift, the doors of the world opened to a little girl from Arkansas who was eager to experience all life had to offer. From that moment on, I knew one of my life's missions was to travel the world, motivating, educating, and helping people become the best that they can be so they too can experience all that life has in store.

Life is fraught with challenges, and my strong resilience has been tested. While at college, I experienced a freak fall down a flight of stairs that resulted in a skull fracture and concussion. I spent quite a bit of time in intensive care, speaking in numbers not words. My weight plummeted to ninety-eight pounds, and I was left with a speech impediment. Most of the time, I didn't know who I was or where I was. Even though the following few years were full of great pain, struggles, and challenges, I persevered and fully recovered.

After graduating college, I was hired by Peter Burwash International (PBI), the world's first and largest International Tennis Management Group, which gave me the opportunity to run and manage tennis programs and facilities and to compete in tournaments at major hotels and resorts in the United States, Austria, Tahiti, Denmark, and Japan. In addition to teaching players nationally and internationally, we hosted numerous charities and donated resources, including free tennis clinics for wheelchair-bound and deaf students in Hawaii.

Plus, I was given the opportunity to star in a tennis television series in Europe, *Tele Tennis*, and later marry Rick Macci. Together we ran the Macci International Tennis Academy and trained top juniors, adults, college, and professional tennis players from around the world, including Venus and Serena Williams, Jennifer Capriati, and Andy Roddick. When with PBI, I played a pro tennis tournament in Tahiti and started helping some of the local players. I was later asked by the Tahitian Tennis Federation to come back and teach some of their top juniors and adults, even though they didn't have the funds to cover my coaching fees. This was a wonderful opportunity for me to give back to the wonderful sport that opened the doors of the world for me.

I presently own and operate three companies: Luxury Properties International (LPI), Legacy Leadership International (LLI), and Joy of Sport (JOS). Developing and managing LPI has been a true labor of love, LLI is an exciting global outreach, and JOS keeps me involved in local, national, and international tennis communities. By offering coaching, consulting, and management, JOS allows me to give back to the sport that has so blessed my life. A percentage of all closings and sales from all three companies (LPI, LLI, and JOS) goes toward creating and funding global charities.

Through my books, videos, and screenplay (*Serendipity of Success, Enjoy: Luxury of Life, Success Stretch,* and *Olympic Heart*) and as an international author, speaker, and life leadership advisor, I have the opportunity to touch people's lives and open doors for others as they were once opened for me.

One of my life's mentors, Zig Ziglar, once said, "You can get anything you want in life, if you help enough other people get what they want." I learned that the secret to enjoying a life of luxury is to live our divine purpose and realize it's not what we get out of life, but what we give that is most important.

My passion and purpose in life is to help people achieve their highest and best levels of joy and success in life by discovering and developing their divine purpose while continually loving, learning, leading, and leaving a Lasting Legacy through Global Giving. With these Secret Keys we can all truly and meaningfully *Enjoy the Luxury of Life!*

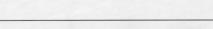

Meet Alexandria Hilton, MA

Living a life of a purpose is living a blessed life. Giving to others, being a contributing member of the community, and giving through charitable work were introduced to me when I was very young. In elementary school, I was taught that every person is on Earth for a purpose and that we are here to make the world a better place.

The role models I was taught to respect and emulate were heroes and heroines who served those in need and who donated their talents for the improvement of humanity. One of those role models was my maternal grandmother. She used to take my sister and me with her as she nursed the ailing members of her community. She brought comfort and healing to her friends and neighbors with joy and enthusiasm when she herself was elderly.

As a family, the ten of us used to visit hospitals on Christmas, singing carols and bringing presents to the patients, especially children. These were our best Christmas celebrations as a family.

Being a competitive athlete was a formative part of my life in Southern California. It became the most satisfying when I combined being a marathon runner with raising money for charity. I ran the Boston Marathon as a qualified runner and raised money for the Hunger Project. For each of the 26.2 miles I ran, sponsors pledged dollars for miles. This was my third marathon and by far the most rewarding!

For over ten years, I was a founding board member for a nonprofit company that organized over twenty community service projects every year. As a pioneer in this sector, I trained the community leaders of the service projects and participated in these projects internationally.

Currently, I am a sponsor for Women for Women International, which provides job training, financial, and emotional support to women who live in regions affected by war. A percentage of the profits from my businesses, Bellissima Consulting (in the US) and EUROUS Global Executive Leadership (international), are donated to charities that support families, health, and the environment.

My lifelong dream has been to be an author, professional speaker, teacher, and trusted advisor to global leaders. As an executive advisor, Master Certified Coach (MCC), and corporate consultant, I work with C-level leaders and senior executives from multinational companies and nonprofit organizations. I am a catalyst for individuals and organizations to discover their true purpose while committing to be global leaders who do what is right for humankind and the environment. My intention is to reveal the human masterpiece in each individual so they can discover how to leave a lasting legacy through Global Giving. To me, that is a life well lived!

When we learn to Give, we start to Live ...

What is Your Gift to Give?